# LADY AND THE TRAMP

LA
A
TRA
Based on Walt Disney
full-length cartoon
This adaptatio
DERRY MOF

# Y
# ND THE
# P

ductions'
re film

y
TT

NEW ENGLISH LIBRARY
TIMES MIRROR

Other stories from Disney cartoon feature films and available in the NEL series

DUMBO
SNOW WHITE AND THE SEVEN DWARFS
SONG OF THE SOUTH
SLEEPING BEAUTY
PINOCCHIO
ROBIN HOOD

**In the whole history of the world there is but one thing that money cannot buy... to wit — the wag of a dog's tail.**

*Josh Billings*

**So it is to all dogs — be they LADIES or TRAMPS — that this book is respectfully dedicated.**



FIRST NEL PAPERBACK EDITION SEPTEMBER 1975
Reprinted October 1975



NEL Books are published by
New English Library Limited from Barnard's Inn, Holborn, London EC1.
Made and printed in Great Britain by
Hunt Barnard Printing Ltd, Aylesbury, Bucks.
Typesetting by The Yale Press Ltd, London SE25

45002686 8

An air of excitement hung over the pretty American mid-west town, for it was Christmas Eve afternoon. Giant snowflakes drifted lazily earthwards, blanketing buildings beneath a dazzling white cover. Lights twinkled invitingly from shop windows piled high with presents. Bells pealed their message of joy and good will from a nearby church.

People trudged through the snow, their faces beaming as they carried gaily wrapped parcels and festive bunches of holly, bright with berries. On a street corner, dressed in a red coat and hat, stood Santa Claus. Snowflakes settled in his beard but he didn't seem to mind. His cheeks were rosy and his eyes sparkled merrily as he called out to passing children and held open his big sack of toys.

Among the jostling crowds, Darling and Jim, a handsome young couple who had married in the summer of that year, were holding hands and laughing as they tried to keep their balance on the slippery ground. A snowflake landed on the tip of Darling's nose. She brushed it away, then said, 'Oh, Jim dear, there's a pet shop! I want to look in the window.'

'Come on then,' replied Jim with a good-natured laugh.

Together they bounded towards it like a pair of playful children and Darling pressed her face to the cold glass. 'Oooohh... just look!' Her voice was filled with delight. 'What an adorable, sweet little puppy. Isn't she the cutest scrap you ever saw?'

'Which one do you mean?' retorted Jim. 'There are five of them curled up together.'

'The little golden spaniel, of course. She's looking right at us. What gorgeous, appealing eyes she has.'

'I agree that she is pretty, but come along, Darling. It's time we went home. Tonight we must finish decorating the tree and we don't want to be out when the carol singers call.'

Reluctantly, Darling turned away from the pet-shop window, the pup's eyes following her accusingly. She was the only pup who was awake and looked so pathetically lonesome and sad. With a toss of red curls, Darling turned her head for a final glimpse of the tiny spaniel before merging with the throng.

Half an hour later, Jim and Darling reached their house.

Jim opened the garden gate and together they walked up the path in the deep, crisp snow. In sharp contrast to the town, the village was quiet and an air of peace and tranquility pervaded the atmosphere.

Attractive houses circled the village green and pond, now frozen over. Children skated on its surface, their happy voices floating on the thin, cold air. In the distance a dog barked and a horse-drawn sleigh moved along the street with a sweet jingling of bells. Trees were silhouetted on neighbouring hills which surrounded the village like a lovely frame. The air had a fresh, clean smell and overhead a large silvery moon hung in the sky resembling a giant lantern.

Darling wrinkled her nose with pleasure and stared up at the stars flashing and twinkling like a thousand jewels against the dark blue curtain of night. 'Jim dear,' she murmured, 'I am so happy. I love this village and our home.'

'So do I.' Jim squeezed her arm affectionately as they walked up the steps of the porch leading to their front door.'We are two very lucky people.' Before going inside, they paused momentarily to gaze again at the Christmas-card scene spread before them, then entered the house, glad of its welcoming warmth.

Later, when Darling was putting the final touches to the Christmas tree, Jim slipped softly out of the house. Darling did not see him go, for she was happily engaged in adding brightly coloured ornaments and tinsel to the tree's branches. At last her task was complete and she stood back to admire her handiwork. A smile of pleasure lit her pretty face, then she ran across to the window to peer out at the houses across the street. They too had trees twinkling and blinking with coloured lights and she clapped her hands with delight. 'It's like Fairyland,' she said aloud. 'Oh... I'd almost forgotten to put Jim's presents under the tree. I wonder where he is?'

Humming a tune, she ran swiftly up the stairs to a cupboard and opening it, brought out several gaily wrapped boxes. She had just placed them beneath the tree when the living room door opened and Jim came in.

'The tree looks lovely,' he said admiringly. His eyes lit on the gifts, each bearing a name tag. He turned to his wife. 'Darling, please go into the other room a minute and promise not to peek.'

'It sound mysterious ... but very exciting,' laughed Darling, walking into the kitchen.

A few minutes later, Jim called her. 'I've put your presents under the tree, Darling, but tonight you can open just one of them.'

'Oh...which shall I choose?' Darling considered the assortment of boxes and packages.

'That one,' smiled Jim, pointing to a hat box tied with scarlet ribbons. Bending over, he picked it up.

'Wow!' retorted Darling. 'It can't be a hat... it seems so heavy. It's sagging at the bottom.' Jim handed her the box and she immediately placed it on the floor and with

trembling fingers, untied the ribbons.

Suddenly the lid rose up and Darling jumped back in astonishment. 'Whatever?' she began in amazement. Then a pair of big brown eyes peeped up at her.

'A present specially for you, Darling. A very merry Christmas.' Jim watched his wife, a happy grin on his face.

'Oh... oh, Jim dear, I can hardly believe it! What a perfectly wonderful gift.' Tears of joy shone in Darling's eyes as she reached inside the box and picked up the tiny golden spaniel pup. 'She's quite irresistible...and wearing such a cute pink ribbon. Thank you - thank you very much.' Raising the puppy on a level with her face she gazed into its eyes. The pup put out her tongue and lovingly licked Darling's cheek. 'She's saying "hullo". How sweet. Stroke her, Jim.'

Gently, Jim caressed the pup. 'You like her, Darling?'

'I love her. What a perfectly beautiful little lady. That's what I'll call her. Lady!'

'A good choice and it suits her. Ah ... listen the carol singers are at the door.'

From the porch, the melodious voices of children singing Christmas songs echoed in the still night air. Jim and Darling listened enraptured and when the carollers had finished, Jim invited them into the house. He gave them candy and mince pies and wished them 'A merry Christmas'. Darling allowed them to stroke Lady who was contented, snuggling warmly in Darling's arms. The tiny pup had found a good mistress and a good home; for her that was the best Christmas present!

Several hours later, Jim glanced at his watch, saying, 'It's getting late, Darling. Time we were off to bed.'

Darling was sitting in an armchair, Lady curled into a small fluffy ball on her lap. 'Where is Lady going to sleep?' she asked.

Jim looked smug. 'That's all arranged.' He went into the hall, returning seconds later with a basket bed. 'I chose it specially. Look how comfortable it is, and there's even a fitted cushion.' He glanced at the puppy. 'She will be very snug.' He stroked Lady's head and she looked up at him briefly, yawned and settled deeper into Darling's lap.

'That won't do, Lady. It's time for you to become acquainted with your *own* bed.' Holding the basket, he walked through to the kitchen, calling Lady to follow.

Darling placed the pup on the floor. For a moment, the tiny spaniel stood still, blinking uncertainly, and then followed Jim through the swinging kitchen door. Its action gently nudged her forward and she slid on the floor's polished surface.

'Easy, girl,' said Jim, laughing. 'Come on...over here.' He patted the basket. 'In you go.'

Lady scampered across to the new basket. She inspected it, licked Jim's hand and defiantly turned her back on her new bed.

'That's not the way of it,' said Jim, scooping Lady into his arms. 'Try this comfortable cushion. It's super... that's a girl.' Gently, he placed Lady inside the basket, covering her with a soft blanket. Immediately, Lady tossed the blanket aside as she struggled to her feet, her long ears flopping.

'No! That won't do. Let's try again.' Jim laid Lady on her back, replacing the blanket.

Darling appeared inside the kitchen doorway. 'Troubles?' she enquired.

'No...not really. We have to get Lady used to the idea, that's all.'

'But Jim dear, she is still a baby. Are you sure that she will be warm enough?'

'Of course!' He glanced down at the pup who was lying motionless but looking indignant. 'She will be as snug as a bug. That basket's a cosy set-up.' He switched off the light. 'Goodnight, Lady,' he called.

'Goodnight,' echoed Darling. Together, they walked through the swing door into the living room.

head, Darling,' urged Jim.

'Lady will go right to sleep and...' He felt a slight tug at the bottom of his pants. He looked down. 'Oh, no, this won't do at all.' The puppy looked up at him, appeal in her eyes.

'Oh, Jim, she's followed us. Isn't that clever!'

'No, Darling, it is not.' Jim picked up Lady, returning her to the kitchen and her basket where he placed her kindly but firmly beneath the cover. 'Now be a good girl. This is where you belong - right here!' Jim hurried from the room. Lady immediately jumped from the basket, obviously not in agreement. Scampering across the shiny floor she pushed her pink button of a nose at the door but it wouldn't move. Following a beam of light glinting from beneath the door, she pushed again. This time she met with success; she had discovered the secret of the swinging door. Pushing again, she hurled herself through with the vigour of a mini-cyclone.

Jim and Darling, arms twined about each other, were making their way up the stairs to bed. A faint whimper made Darling turn round. 'Oh, Jim...look! She's so lonesome. Don't you think that maybe... just for tonight...'

'Now, Darling, if we are going to show her who's master, we must be firm from the beginning.' Jim raced downstairs, plucked Lady off the first stair and resolutely returned her to her basket. Alone, feeling rejected, Lady commenced to howl, cry and whimper in turn.

'Lady, stop that now. Cut it out!'

The little pup blinked and looked around for the owner of the voice. No one was in the kitchen but a loud pounding came from overhead and the kitchen light was swaying. Her puppy mind worked quickly. Darling was up that long flight of stairs in the room above. She would try again.

The kitchen door wasn't easy for her to open and for a while she stood close to it, whimpering and shivering. If she cried for a long time, perhaps help would come. It did - but not exactly the sort of help she was looking for. An irate Jim, clad in pyjamas, entered the kitchen and switched on the light. Pointing to the basket, he said angrily, 'Back to bed at once. Go along... quickly now ...and I don't want to hear another whimper ... not a sound.' Sadly, Lady padded back to the unwelcome basket and climbed in.

Jim returned to the bedroom, and for a while Lady lay without moving, but her mind was busy. She was not prepared to admit defeat. It would be imprudent to make an immediate move - but if she waited a little while. She settled down temporarily, while outside the window, snow continued to fall like a giant white eiderdown and Christmas day drew closer. In the hall, the grandfather clock ticked away the minutes. When it sonorously boomed the hour of two, Lady felt it was time to make another move. With some difficulty she made her exit from the kitchen and reached the bottom of the flight of stairs. They were long and steep and Lady viewed them with dismay. It would be a

strenuous climb. However, there was no point in wasting time thinking about it.

Laboriously, she began to pull herself up one stair after another. It was a difficult struggle and she kept pausing to rest. But finally, effort was rewarded and she found herself in the upper hall. She paused again. One of the doors was slightly open and presently, Lady peered inside. A large bed stood in the centre of the room. She padded towards it but retreated when she heard strange noises. Closer investigation showed that Jim was snoring. On the opposite side of the bed, Darling was asleep, one hand resting outside the covers. Lady placed her paws on the quilt, licked Darling's hand and started whimpering. It went as planned.

Immediately, Darling woke up. 'You little precious... you climbed those big stairs all by yourself. What a clever girl.' Reaching over, she drew Lady onto the bed.

Jim sleepily opened his eyes. 'Were you talking to me?' he murmured.

'No, Jim dear. It's Lady. She's climbed all the way up and...'

Right on cue, Lady dashed across the covers and licked Jim's face, crying softly. Her doggie mind knew that *this* was the moment. If she was returned again to her basket, she was fighting a lost cause - but if she could win Jim over... Employing all her wiles, she licked his eyelids and cheeks, whimpering, pleading pathetically.

'Aw... all right,' said Jim, softening. 'But remember, Darling, it's just for tonight!'

'Oh, thank you, Jim honey. She won't be any trouble, you'll see.' Darling placed Lady snugly on the over coverlet and stroked her. With a blissful sigh, Lady settled down to sleep. Her worries were over. The battle had been won!

Almost six months had passed since the Christmas Eve when Lady had first entered Jim and Darling's life. Now, she was an accepted member of the family. Life was good and she was happy. She never felt tired or hungry and she loved her master and mistress with true doggie devotion. The clutching fingers of winter had long since given way to mid-summer. Gone were the muffled sounds of horses' hooves pulling sleighs across the frozen ground, and the clear timbre of children's voices as they skated and played their wintry games.

Spring had been a short but brilliant season when the garden at the back of the house had been a froth of colour. Pink and white flowers, delicate as mist, had nudged stabs of yellow bloom, making a sharp contrast to the vivid blue sky. Now, in the fullness of summer, the garden was equally delightful... not to mention the village pond. In its waters lived a family of ducks and an assortment of tiny fish; weeds grew around its edge and were a source of delight to

Lady. She loved to conceal herself behind their cover and bark at the unsuspecting ducks. They usually clucked their annoyance and swam rapidly away, but Lady really loved her feathered neighbours.

It was six o'clock in the morning. The clock on the mantelpiece had just chimed the hour. Lady stretched lazily and sat up on the pale-green silk coverlet on the bed. Dawn had long since brushed the skies with her first rosy hues and through the partially opened curtains Lady could see golden sunlight slanting on the tree outside the window. The tree was covered with tiny, hard green apples and when the wind blustered through the garden sprinkling the unripe fruit onto the grass, Lady delighted in playing with it.

The air was filled with birdsong and as Lady yawned again, a blackbird flew into the branches of the apple tree and burst into a silvery cadence of sweet melody.

Lady blinked, licked Darling's face, then jumped onto the floor. Yes... it was a grand day and time to be up. Running around the foot of the bed, she licked Jim's hand for it was hanging outside the covers. He didn't stir so she placed her cold pink nose beneath the sheet, found his toe and tugged gently at it until Jim woke up.

He sat up with a start. 'It's all right, Lady. Take it easy, girl I'm awake. Whatever time is it? I'm getting up... okay... I'm up.' Jim stumbled unsteadily to his feet and rubbed his eyes. He glanced at the clock. 'Oh dear, Lady... you've done it again.'

'Done what again? What's wrong, Jim?' Darling's voice was a sleepy question.

Jim staggered back to bed, pulling the covers about his ears. 'Can't you explain to Lady about Sundays? She continues to insist that I go to work seven days a week.' He yawned. 'I'm for forty more winks.'

Lady scampered round the bed to her mistress. 'Go along... good girl... into the garden.' Affectionately, she watched Lady dash towards the bedroom door, then she too, snuggled back beneath the covers.

Lady bounded down the stairs and went through her own private swinging door into the garden. The grass was covered with pearly dew and blackbirds dug into the lawn hopefully searching for worms. With a loud, delighted bark, Lady chased them away and

they perched together on the delicate branches of a weeping willow tree cheeping their disapproval. Spying a bone which she had tucked away behind a bush on the previous evening, Lady dragged it over to the tulip bed and commenced to dig a hole in which to bury it. Earth flew in all directions, so did a tulip. Knowing that Jim would be annoyed, because for some peculiar reason best known to humans, he disapproved of his flowers being dug up, Lady promptly replanted the flower. Unfortunately, she planted it upside down and then unconcernedly bounded away.

At the end of the garden close to a shed, stood a wood-pile. Throughout most of the year Jim, in his spare moments, sawed long timbers into neat, even-sized logs. He stacked them ready for use in the cold weather. But the wood-pile was a great attraction for rats and Lady kept a vigilant eye each day to see that none of them lurked there. A slight movement caught her sharp eyes and on closer investigation, she spied a rat glaring at her from beneath the wood-pile.

With a triumphant bark, Lady leapt towards it. Cornered, the rat emerged, standing menacingly on its hind feet. Lady growled, a low threatening sound, and advanced. The rat had second thoughts about bravery and scampered back beneath the wood and out on the other side. Hot in pursuit, Lady dashed round the shed, but she was too late. The rat had disappeared through a hole in the fence. Frustrated, Lady dug frenziedly at the hole in an attempt to enlarge it but the sound of a bicycle bell made her pause in her endeavours.

The local newspaper boy came riding along the street, whistling a gay tune and tossing newspapers with accurate aim onto front porches. Like a catapult, Lady dashed for *her* front garden and was in time to catch the well aimed paper.

'Good catch, Lady,' called the boy cheerfully as he continued on down the street.

Lady carried the newspaper round the corner of the house and up the back steps to her private swing door. She made two vain attempts to enter but the newspaper was too wide for the door. Finally, she backed in but a loud tearing sound indicated that all had not gone well. The paper was badly torn.

Jim and Darling were having breakfast. Unabashed by her slight accident, Lady placed the paper at Jim's feet. 'Clever girl,' he told her absent-mindedly as he sipped coffee. He reached for the paper, opened it up and sighed, 'Look... she's done it again.'

Darling burst out laughing. 'Never mind, Jim. She does try to please and she's so adorable.'

Jim thrust his hand through the giant tear in the paper. 'There's one point in her favour, Darling. Have you noticed that since she personally undertook to deliver our paper to the breakfast table, we see less and less of those disturbing headlines? The "doom and gloom" bridgade don't stand a chance round here.'

'Yes! Come to think of it, that's true. How did we ever get along without Lady?' Darling held a large doughnut under the table as Jim poured coffee into his saucer and put it on the floor. With a bark of thanks, Lady took the doughnut, dunked it in the saucer of coffee and ate it with enjoyment. When it was finished, she lapped up the remainder of the coffee.

Darling looked at her pet with admiring eyes. 'Jim, she's grown into such a beautiful dog. Such a proud, intelligent head and as for her coat, its the envy of all the other dog-owners in the village. She is an aristocrat... a true Lady.'

Jim nodded agreement. 'Say, she must be six months old by now. It's time we were getting her a dog licence.'

'Heavens, yes. And a collar, too!'

Jim held out his cup. 'Is there anything left in the percolator?' Darling poured more coffee and he continued, 'I'll see to that business when I'm downtown tomorrow.'

Two days later, Darling walked into the living room and called Lady. Eagerly, she bounded in from the kitchen. 'Look, Lady, I've got something for you,' said Darling holding a package under Lady's nose. Gently, she sniffed the brown wrapping but it didn't tell her anything. Sitting up on her haunches she watched curiously as Darling untied the string.

It's a present for you,' Darling told her. 'Come and look.' Darling lifted a handsome blue collar studded with tiny gems from its wrappings. 'Do you like it?' She held the collar out towards Lady. Her eyes brightened with recognition. Some of her doggy friends who lived along the street wore collars, but not as nice as this one. She bounded forward.

'Hope it fits,' exclaimed Darling, fastening it round Lady's neck. It felt a little strange and Lady stretched her neck and shook her head. Darling took a small mirror from the wall and held it in front of Lady. 'There - see how nice it looks. And so grown up. Jock and Trusty will be surprised when they see you today. Go along... show your scottie friend what a grand Lady you are now.'

With a delighted 'woof', Lady jumped up to lick Darling's hands and then rushed on to the front porch. She would make a call or two. Elegantly, she walked down her front path, through the gate and over to a neighbouring garden.

Jock, a proud black scottie, lived next door. He was engaged in adding yet another succulent bone to his already ample supply. Carrying the bone in his mouth, every now and then he looked suspiciously about him. It wouldn't do for Trusty, the bloodhound, to find his buried treasure. Or Lady either, for that matter. Even though she was a gentle, refined creature and he could not imagine her trying to steal anything from anyone. And yet... one never knew. It didn't pay to be too trusting. Humming a tune, he bounded down the path in leaps and turned into some bushes.

Four steps ahead, then to the left,
And right to the place where I marked it,
With a bonnie bone,
That I'll bury for my own...

He broke off as he came to a clearing beyond the bushes and vigorously commenced to dig. Soon he had uncovered a deep hole packed full of bones. He dropped the latest addition in with the others. 'In my bonnie bonnie bank in my own back yard.' Gazing in admiration at his handiwork he said aloud. 'Aye, that's a grand sight.'

Someone called his name. Jock pricked up his ears. 'That sounds like Lady. I must cover up my treasure.' Quickly, he jumped onto the hole, covering the bones as he sat down. Admittedly, his posture was a trifle uncomfortable-looking, for the bones were scratchy, but he had to protect his interests.

'Jock,' called Lady again. 'Ah...there you are.' She pranced towards Jock, her collar jingling. 'Hullo, Jock. Aren't you going to speak to me today?'

Jock looked perturbed. He didn't want to remain seated on the bones, but on the other hand it wouldn't be prudent to leave them exposed for all and sundry to see. 'Oh...oh...it's you, my bonnie lassie. I'll be with you in a minute.' Trying to appear nonchalant, he scraped dirt over the hole.

Lady, proud of her new collar scarcely appeared to notice Jock's furtive action. 'See anything different?' she asked.

Jock looked up briefly from his task. 'Eh? Oh...you've had a bath!'

'No...not that,' said Lady impatiently. 'I had a bath yesterday.'

Jock flicked more dirt across the ground. 'Then you've had your nails clipped.'

'No! No!' said Lady restlessly. 'Guess again.' She circled the hole concealing the bones, jingling her collar again.

Jock's task was almost complete and he heaved a sigh of relief. Why did females arrive at inconvenient moments? 'Well...I...I guess I would'na be knowin' then.'

'Oh!' Lady looked very disappointed as she drew closer to Jock.

'Why, my bonnie lassie,' he said sniffing the new leather, 'It's a collar...a bonnie, brand new collar.'

'Do you like it?'

'Aye! Hmmm... by the look of it, it must have been verra expensive!' Jock was not given to being over-expressive.

Lady tossed her head. 'My folks are very good to me.'

'Yes - indeed they are. Have you shown it to Trusty yet?'

'No! You're my closest neighbour and I wanted you to be the first to know of my good fortune.'

'Aye, lass. I appreciate that, but we'd best go to Trusty's at once. You know how sensitive he can be about such things.'

Further along the street there stood a pleasant house with an iron grill fence and a roomy front porch. Together, Lady and Jock trotted in its direction, hoping they would find Trusty at home.

'Just as I thought...' remarked Jock with a

snort as he and Lady ambled up the front path towards the porch. 'He's asleep.'

'And dreaming,' laughed Lady. 'Just look at his nose twitching. Look... now a caterpillar has crawled onto it.'

Trusty, a large bloodhound, suddenly jerked his head and the caterpillar fell onto the porch. Lady and Jock padded up the porch steps. 'Aye! Trusty is doubtless dreaming of those bonnie bygone days when

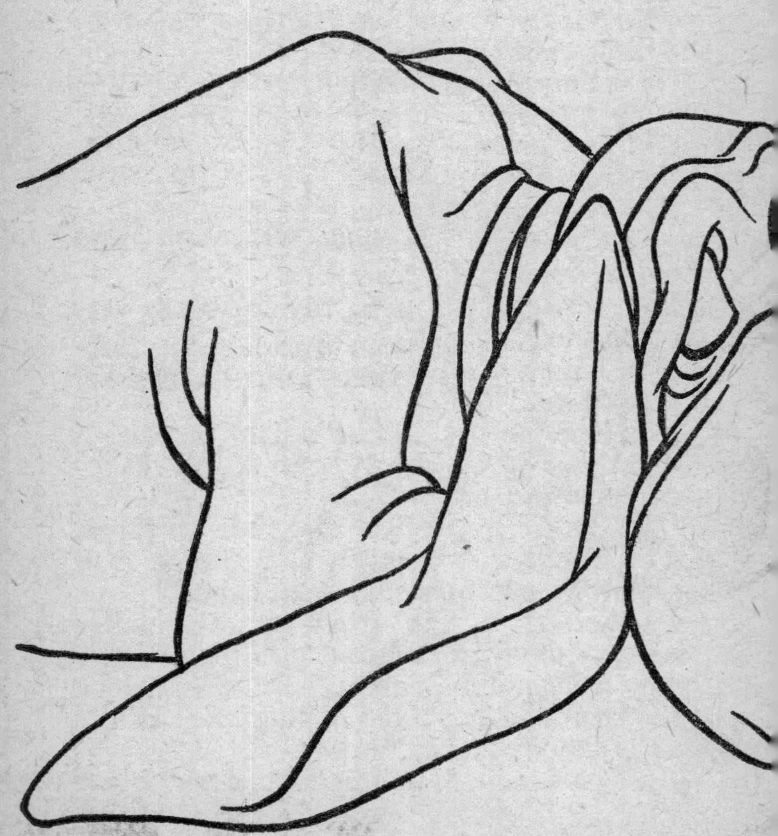

he and his grandfather were trackin' criminals through the swamps.'

'They were?' Lady's big brown eyes lit up with interest.

'Yes...but that was before...'

'Before what?' asked Lady, full of curiousity.

Jock looked doleful. 'Tis time you knew the truth, lassie.' He glanced at his old pal to make sure that he couldn't overhear. The caterpillar had escaped into a knothole and Trusty, in his dreams, was looking for it. 'See,' said Jock, 'he should be able to find that furry creature with ease but...' He shook his head sadly. 'It shouldna' happen to a dog, but well - Trusty has lost his sense of smell!'

Lady gasped her dismay. 'Oh, no! How awful!'

'Aye, it is indeed!' Jock placed his head close to Lady's ear. 'But we must never let on that

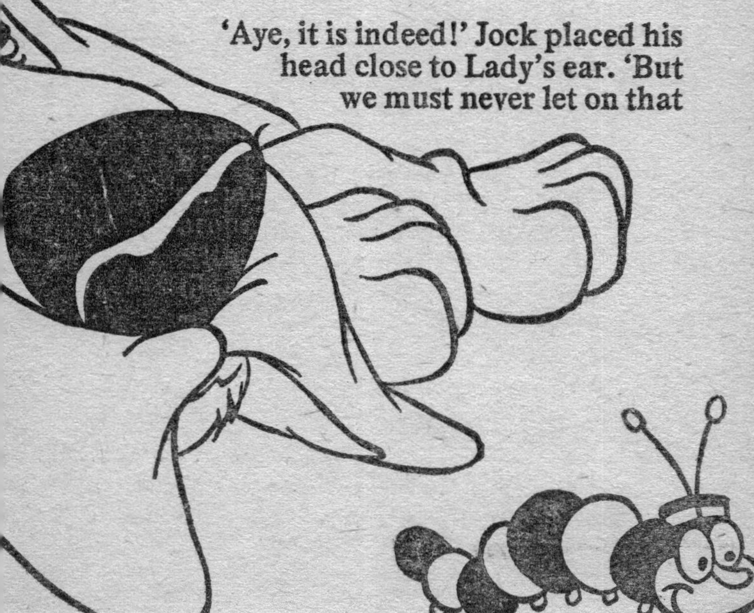

we know... it would break his heart.'

Trusy, still sniffing, woke up. 'Hi, you two. Excuse me a moment. I've lost something. Which way did he go?'

Jock pretended to look puzzled. 'Go?' he asked.

'Yeah! A big fellow.' Trusty rolled his bloodshot eyes. 'He was about six foot two... may be three. Wore a striped suit.'

Jock and Lady exchanged puzzled glances. Lady shook her golden shoulders.

'He wasn't wearing a collar. Surely you saw him!' Trusty sounded plaintive. 'Why, Miss Lady,' he suddenly observed, '*You* have a collar! That's wonderful. And it's so smart, too.'

Lady tried to look nonchalant. 'Uh huh... and I've a licence.'

'My, my.' Trusty shook his large head. 'How time does fly.'

Jock sat down close to Trusty. 'Aye! It seems only yesterday that she was cutting her teeth on Jim's slippers...and now...there she is, a full-grown Lady.'

Aware of the favourable impression that she was creating, Lady stepped over to Trusty's water bowl and daintily took a drink. Trusty scrutinised his own collar. 'Yes. It's grand to be wearing the greatest honour a man can bestow.'

Jock walked over to Lady. 'The badge of faith and respectability,' he said. Lady licked a few reamining drops of moisture from her chin.

'That's right, Miss Lady.' Trusty thrust his face in the direction of his friends. 'As my grandpappy, Ol' Reliable, used to say... Don't recollect if I've ever mentioned Ol' Reliable before...'

'Aye, you have, laddie.' Jock tried not to sound bored. He and Lady had both heard tales of Trusty's grandpappy many times over.

'Oh!' Trusty looked taken aback. 'I don't recollect having mentioned it but I guess...'

A long, shrill whistle pierced the air and immediately, Lady pricked up her ears. 'It's Jim Dear. I must go. Please excuse me.' With a short, triumphant bark she dashed down the porch steps and tore after Jim, who was walking along the street.

'Hullo there, Lady. Come on, I'll beat you home!' Jim fondled Lady's ears then raced towards the garden gate.

Lady easily won the race and when Jim reached the porch, she was waiting for him and sitting up daintily, begging for a titbit. He placed it on her nose. Proudly she held it there, waiting for him to admire her new collar. 'That's a girl. You won again. Say... what have we here?' His eyes alighted on her new adornment. 'Very chic! You're really grown up now.'

Joyfully, Lady flung the titbit in the air catching it with the ease of an expert. Jim opened the front door and stood aside. 'Come along. Today is very special...Ladies first.' Lady pranced into the entrance hall feeling like a queen.

During the sunny afternoon, Jim cut the grass while Lady scampered delightedly among the flower beds, chasing birds and dodging in and out of the mignonette and poppies. Her nose was bright yellow with pollen from thrusting it deep into the blooms. The air was sweet with warm summer scents and life was good. Afternoon slipped into evening and a cool breeze ruffled the birds' feathers and the sun dipped in the western sky.

'It's time for supper,' called Jim to Lady whose attention was now devoted to the wood-pile. 'And it smells good. Come along.' After Jim had put the garden tools away, they raced eagerly for the house. Lady's nose twitched expectantly for the appetising smell drifting from the kitchen told her that chicken was on the menu.

Later that evening when the supper dishes had been washed, Lady lay curled in a contented ball at Jim and Darling's feet. She yawned, stretching luxuriously. Her tummy was full and she was ready to call it a day. Jim leaned over, patting her and scratching her chin. Lady wagged her tail in response and then resettled herself more comfortably across Jim's slippered feet. With a gentle sigh, she closed her eyes.

Darling laughed. 'She's as adorable as ever. The nicest Christmas present I've ever had.'

'You know, Darling,' remarked Jim, 'with Lady here, I'd say our life is quite complete. What more could we want?'

Snuggling close, Darling rested her head on Jim's shoulder. 'I agree with you, dear. I can't imagine anything ever taking her place in our hearts.'

Way beyond the village, and on the outskirts of the mid-west town where Jim had purchased Lady, lay the railway tracks. All day long, and often far into the night, noisy trains shunted back and forth. Snooty people usually referred to the area as the 'wrong side of town' and avoided it like the plague.. For others, it was a friendly place and as far as Tramp was concerned, it was right for him.

Tramp was a medium-sized dog of indeterminate breed and noted amongst the dog fraternity as being stubborn, brave and defiant. Nobody's fool, Tramp knew his way around and could take care of himself. Although he belonged to nobody in particular, in another sense he belonged to many people. He had friends in places that mattered...mainly cafes and restaurants not far from the railway. He visited them all in turn but kept his independence. That was the way he preferred to live.

Tramp was asleep in a barrel-like part of a water tower, close to the tracks. He

breathed in regular rhythm to the tempo of a steam train shunting close by. But it was already daylight and other noises filtered in from the streets disturbing him. Tramp opened one eye, yawned, then got slowly to his feet. Emerging from the barrel he stretched, walked over to a puddle and took a long drink. Then he had a brief shower beneath a dripping water pipe and shook himself vigorously.

'Brrr!' he muttered. 'That was chilly. What a day! Well, now to dig up some breakfast.'

He strutted along on the alert with his head cocked. Tramp could not be described as a handsome dog, yet he radiated appeal. Certainly, female dogs found his attentions flattering...he was so strong and protective. His shaggy coat was a mixture of brown and beige; he had high shoulders, a yellow glint in his bright eyes, a black nose and a very powerful set of white teeth as many a luckless victim knew. But right now, trouble was not on Tramp's mind, but food. As he scampered along, he noticed some puppies for sale in a pet shop window. He paused to stare at them through the glass, pity in his eyes. One of them jumped up, barking excitedly, trying to lick Tramp through the

glass. 'They're cute little rascals,' he said. 'Coochie coochie coochie coo. Hmmmm...I sure hope they make out all right.'

Tramp turned away from the window. It didn't pay to get too sentimental. 'Now, where to?' he wondered. 'Let's see. Shall I go to Bernie's?' He thought about it for a moment. 'Hmmm... I wonder. There's François Pastries across the street. They're pretty good...but no! Too much starch in buns. I'd rather have meat today.' His eyes roved further along the block. 'Ah...Tony's place. That's it. I haven't been there in a week.'

Tramp crossed the street, walked down a side alley and scratched loudly on a Dutch door. Inside the restaurant, the rich tenor

voice of a man singing filled the morning air. Tramp scratched again. Suddenly the door opened and a short, thick-set man with black hair and a kindly face looked out. A wide grin lit up his face when he noticed his visitor.

'Well, Butch, old boy...long time no see. You wanna' your breakfast, eh?'

Tramp jumped up, prancing on his back legs and showing off for his Italian friend. 'Okay,' went on the kindly man. 'We've been expectin' you and the bossa...he's a sava some nicea bones for you.'

Tramp barked approval and jumped down ready to catch a large, juicy bone. Holding it between his strong teeth he wagged his tail in thanks and trotted off. Curling up behind a fence, he settled down to enjoy his breakfast. A noise distracted his attention...a noise with which he was familiar. Crouching lower, he glared ferociously between the slats of the fence.

Parked across the street was the dog-catcher's wagon. Peering dismally from behind its bars were two luckless dogs. Tramp was wise to the ways of wily dog-catchers and avoided them whenever possible. But on occasion, some of his more foolish friends had the misfortune to be caught, and were locked up in quarters which even the toughest of them agreed left a great deal to be desired.

Tramp peered again. Yes...there was the dog-catcher nailing a notice onto the fence. Impatiently, Tramp waited until the man had moved away then he read the notice. As

he had guessed, it was bad news all the way.

WARNING. NOTICE IS HEREBY GIVEN THAT ANY UNLICENSED DOG WILL BE IMMEDIATELY IMPOUNDED. BY ORDER OF THE CITY COUNCIL.

Tramp growled low in his throat. He should keep well out of sight...but on the other hand, two of his buddies were already in the wagon. Tramp dashed across the street and jumped onto the back step of the van. 'Hey! Pssst!,' he called trying to attract the attention of a melancholy bulldog.

The bulldog looked up without enthusiasm, saw Tramp and immediately brightened. 'Blimey! Look, Peg,' he said addressing the other imprisoned dog, 'It's de Tramp!'

'Shhhhhh!' warned Tramp. 'The dog-catcher is not far away.'

'Hi ya, handsome!' said Peg, a cheeky creature with a long, silky coat. 'Come to join the party?' She waggled her tail with a saucy air.

'All right, all right, you two. Cut the wise-cracks... there isn't time. I'll try to get you out.' Tramp attempted to open the latch on the barred door while keeping a wary eye open for the dog-catcher. 'They tell me the pressure's really on,' he growled. 'Signs posted all over town.' The latch gave under his expert pressure. 'Quick - move,' he said.

The two grateful dogs jumped down the steps to freedom. 'Gee, thanks,' said Peg with a cheeky wink.

'You're a bit of all right, chum,' growled the bulldog. 'I won't forget this.' Footsteps were approaching and he and Peg vanished behind the fence. They had no intention of being taken a second time.

But the dog-catcher arrived quickly on the scene and Tramp found himself in a dangerous position. 'Get going,' yelled Tramp to his pals. 'Scram...and be careful.'

'Hey! what the heck's going on?' The dog-catcher, his face contorted with fury, made a dive towards Tramp. But Tramp was ready and nipped him sharply on the leg. The man yelled. 'Why, you mangy mutt - let go! Let go of me! I'll get you for this!'

Tramp relinquished his hold then dashed frenziedly across the street, jumping over a wall. The dog-catcher gave chase but he was no match for Tramp. He gave up running and stood shaking his fist at the furry brown-and-beige dynamo. 'Darned dog,' he muttered. 'I'll get him yet...I sure will.' From his hiding place, Tramp grinned.

He waited till the coast was clear, his mind active. The railway tracks would be pretty unhealthy for the next few days; that dog-catcher didn't give up easily. He'd be back tomorrow...and the next day...and the next.

Tramp came to a sudden decision. Turning in the direction of the pretty village on the far side of town, he sniffed the air appreciatively. 'Hmm... Snob Hill, here I come,' he said, stepping out with a jaunty air. 'For a while at least, I'll see how the other half lives.'

Morning, warm beneath a velvet blue sky, was wearing on when Tramp finally reached the pretty village where Lady lived. He eyed the select street lined with trees, their leaves already tinged with the first bright shades of autumn. Tramp strolled across to a water trough close to the village green and drank deeply. He was hot and thirsty from his long walk.

Pigeons pecked at the ground, their heads bobbing. 'Hi, girls. How's pickings? Pretty slim, eh?' The pigeons ignored Tramp's comment and when he approached them, flew away.

Tramp shrugged his high shoulders. 'Hmmmm...even the pigeons are stuck-up. I'll bet they've got a lid on every dustbin round here...and a fence around every tree. Snobsville, indeed!'

He crossed the street. 'Huh... wonder what the leash and collar set does for excitement?'

Trusty the bloodhound, accompanied by Jock, was making a call on Lady. Three months had passed since the special day when she had proudly shown her friends her new jewel-studded collar. Three happy months...but now...

'Lassie! Lassie!' called Jock as he and Trustv ambled up the front garden path.

'Oh, Miss Lady, ma'am!' Trusty was noted for his polite southern manners.

There was no reply to their greetings. 'That's odd,' remarked Jock. 'She always rushes to meet us.' Rounding the corner of the house he saw Lady lying dejectedly by her dish of food. Birds pecked at the contents but Lady ignored them 'Ah! Good morning, Lassie. 'Tis a bonnie, braw, bright day...uh... what's all this?'

Lady gazed sadly at her two friends, her big brown eyes filled with unshed tears.

'Why, Miss Lady,' said Trusty kindly. 'Is...ah...somethin' wrong?'

Jock looked around with a belligerent expression then scratched the ground with his hind feet. 'Aye...you tell us, Lassie. If somebody's been mistreatin'...'

Lady's gloomy expression turned to one of puzzlement. 'Oh, no, Jock. It's something I've done, I guess.'

'You?' Trusty looked amazed.

'It must be.' Lady sighed and glanced up towards the open window. Inside, Darling was humming contentedly. 'Jim Dear and Darling are acting so... so strangely.'

Darling came to the window and placed a newly potted plant on the sill. She didn't appear to notice the three dogs but went on singing. Lady looked hurt then rushed round to the greenhouse.

With a shrug, Jock said to Trusty, 'We'd best find out what this is all about.'

In the greenhouse, the three friends sat down together. 'Now, Lassie,' commenced Jock, 'let us have the details.'

Lady sighed, then said in a small voice, 'I first noticed it the other day when Jim Dear came home. It was five o'clock and I was standing on the window-seat waiting to greet him. He came through the front gate and I rushed out. Instead of fondling me as he usually does, he ignored me and raced towards the house. I followed, jumping all the way but he turned on me sharply and ordered, "Down, Lady... down!" '

A sad tear trickled down her golden furry nose. 'I just couldn't believe my ears.' She paused a moment to recover her composure then continued. 'Jim dashed into the house calling loudly for Darling. When she appeared he asked, "Are you all right?" She laughed and said, "Why shouldn't I be?" He looked concerned. "Well, sweet... I just can't help worrying. After all, in your condition, alone here all day and walking that dog..." '

'Walking that dog?' repeated Jock, in shocked tones.

'That dog?' Trusty looked dismayed, his bloodshot eyes rolling in disbelief.

Lady lowered her nose onto velvety paws.

'Oh...the hurt... the humiliation. He's *never* called me that before.'

Jock couldn't understand it all. Whatever words of comfort could he offer? 'Well, now, Lassie...don't fret yourself. I wouldna worry my wee head about it. Remember... they're only humans after all.'

'As my Grandpappy, Ol' Reliable used to say,' cut in Trusty 'Er... don't recollect if I've ever mentioned Ol' Reliable before...'

Jock sighed. 'Aye, you have laddie. Frequently!'

Lady sat up. 'And now, Darling is acting so strangely. We've always enjoyed our afternoon romp together, but yesterday, I carried my leash into the living room, where Darling was knitting. I looked up at her expentantly for it was a gorgeous afternoon, but she picked up my leash and said, "No, Lady. No walk today." I thought that she wanted to play games instead so I found my rubber ball. She took that away, too and said in a firm voice, "No... no... not now!" '

'Then...' and Lady's voice dropped to a mere whisper, 'I tugged at her knitting yarn and she almost screamed at me to drop it. I was holding it in my mouth and she got up and actually... actually spanked me.' Her voice broke and this time the tears flowed down Lady's nose, trickling onto the greenhouse floor to form a tiny puddle. Jock and Trusty exchanged meaningful glances that Lady could not interpret. 'It's not that I was hurt... not really! More a matter of my pride. You see, Darling had never struck me before.'
never struck me before.'

To Lady's amazement, Jock's shaggy black face broke into a grin. 'Ha! Ha! Now dinna take it too seriously, lassie; after all, at a time like this...'

'Yes,' cut in Trusty. 'You see, Miss Lady, there comes a time in the life of all humans when...as they put it, the birds and the bees...or...er...well, the stork...you understand? No?'

Clearly, Lady didn't understand. 'What he's trying to say, Lady,' cut in Jock, 'is that Darling is expecting a wee bairn.'

'Bairn?' questioned Lady, looking confused.

'He means a baby,' explained Trusty.

As Jock prepared to explain further,

Tramp came trotting past Lady's garden. At the sight of the trio, he paused, peeking round the gate-post, then sat down watching Lady with admiration. The drift of the conversation floated to his interested ears. Jock went on talking to Lady. 'Well... babies...they resemble humans.'

'But ah'd say a mite smaller,' interrupted Trusty.

'Aye! And they walk on all fours.' Jock was determined to have his say.

'And,' added Trusty sagely, 'if I remember correctly, they beller a lot.'

'Aye! And they're verra expensive. You'll no be permitted to play wi' it.' Jock looked mournful.

'But,' murmured Trusty, 'They're mighty sweet.'

'And verra, verra soft,' added his pal.

This intriguing conversation was too much for Tramp. He decided to join in so he strolled over to the group.

'Just a cute little bundle... ah... of trouble.'

Lady turned her head and stared at the stranger. Pleased that he had her attention, Tramp continued, 'Yeah! They scratch pinch, pull ears... aw, but shucks, any dog can take that. It's what they do to your happy home...'

Jock and Trusty glared at the intruder but he didn't seem in the least perturbed. Pushing Jock aside, Tramp squeezed in next to Lady, saying to Jock, 'Move over, will ya, friend?'

Jock scowled his annoyance, but Tramp continued talking, staring into Lady's lovely brown eyes. 'Home-wreckers... that's what babies are!'

'Look here, laddie, who are you to barge in and...' Jock's voice trembled with anger at this strange dog's impudence.

'The voice of experience, Buster.' Jock's wrath failed to make an impression on Tramp as he went on, 'Huh, huh, boy. Just wait till junior get here. You get the urge for a nice, comfortable scratch and... "Put that dog out!" they yell. "He'll get fleas all over the baby." You start barking at some strange mutt, it's "Stop that racket! You'll wake the baby!" ' Tramp sighed, lying down in front of Lady. 'And then...' he went on, '...then they hit you in the room-and-board department.' He paused a moment, visualising a thick beefsteak. 'Oh,' he said, his mouth watering, 'remember those nice juicy cuts of beef? Forget 'em. Leftover baby food. And that nice warm bed by the fire? A leaky doghouse!'

'Oh dear...oh dear...' Lady looked very distressed.

Jock jumped to his feet. 'Dinna listen, lassie. No human is that cruel.'

'Of course not.' Trusty moved closer. 'Miss Lady, everybody knows a dog's best friend is his human!'

Tramp rolled over on the ground, doubled up with laughter. 'Oh, come on now, fellas. Oh! You surely haven't fallen for that old line... now have you?'

'Aye! And we've no need for mongrels and their r... r... radical ideas!' Jock was furious. 'Off with ye noo! Off with ye! Off with ye!'

'Okay, Sandy!'

Tramp looked insolent.

'Okay.,. Jock.'

Jock glared aggressively. 'Heather Lad O' Glencairn to you!' he said pompously, giving himself his full title.

'Okay, okay, okay!' Tramp wasn't looking for a fight.

He walked back to Lady's side. 'But remember, Pigeon. A human heart has only so much room for love and affection.' With a shrug, he turned towards the garden gate, ready to depart. 'When a baby moves in, the dog moves out.'

Tramp's gloomy prediction was just too much. Lady dissolved again into a flood of tears.

Autumn's gay scarves of colour gradually faded, giving way to winter again. The trees stood naked, bereft of leafy splendour; the pond once more was frozen over. Life for Lady remained pleasant though Jim and Darling did not devote quite as much time to her amusement as they had done in the past. Darling continued to knit tiny wool garments and each afternoon she rested on the sofa.

Lady accepted that long walks and romping on the village green were out unless she went on her own. She continued to be well fed and though she could no longer sleep each night on the bed, her basket was allowed to stay in the bedroom. Perhaps Jock and Trusty had been mistaken in their assumptions.

When Spring brightened the hedgerows, trees came into fresh bud and birds sang lustily as if their hearts would burst, Lady's fears were laid to rest. She was a little puzzled by the amount of women who called on Darling, fussing over her as if she was an invalid, while insisting that she looked radiant.

Presents also began to pile up. Rattles, bootees, bonnets and hosts of tiny garments. Lady examined them with interest, then dismissed them from her mind. Then one day, in the month of April, there was a freak thunderstorm. Lightning flashed and rain knifed the window-panes. Darling looked pale and unwell and phoned Jim who was at work.

He rushed home, his face taut and set in worried lines. A little while later, the local doctor arrived in his buggy and dashed upstairs to the bedroom where Darling lay groaning. During this tense time, Lady was completely ignored and she knew better than to get in the way. Lying on a cushion in the kitchen, she felt rejected and lonely.

A great shout of joy from the living room made her stir and she ran in to see what was happening. Jim was speaking on the telephone, his face radiant with joy. 'Yes, Aunt Sarah... it's a boy... a boy! isn't that wonderful! Just what we wanted. The nursery is all ready. I can't tell you how thrilled we both are.'

Lady listened to this odd conversation with ears cocked. 'A boy,' she reflected. 'It must be something extra special. Jim has never looked so pleased or excited - ever!'

A thin wailing sound floated downstairs from the room above. Whatever was that unfamiliar noise? Lady shook her head. 'I just can't understand,' she thought. 'It must be something wonderful... something grand.

'Cause everybody's smiling in a kind and wistful way. And they haven't even noticed that I'm around today.'

Creeping up to the first landing, Lady paused for a while, peering through the stained glass window overlooking the garden. Jim dashed past carrying a tray and whistling merrily. He didn't even notice Lady.

'It's no good,' Lady told herself. 'I've just got to find out for myself.' Cautiously, she made her way to the partially opened bedroom door. Peering inside, she saw Darling propped up in bed, her eyes alight with happiness as she crooned softly to a tiny human scrap held snug in her arms. Darling looked so happy that Lady couldn't help smiling. Sitting quietly she listened to Darling sing a lullaby:

La la lu, la la lu,
Oh my little star sweeper
I'll sweep the stardust for you.
La la lu, la la lu,
Little soft fluffy sleeper
Here comes a pink cloud for you,
La la lu, la la lu,
Little wandering angel,
Fold up your wings,
Close your eyes,
La la lu, la la lu,
And may love be your keeper,
La la lu, la la lu.
There now, little star sweeper,
Dream on!

Softly, Lady padded across to the bed, then Jim came in, and together he and Lady admired the baby who had now been settled into his cradle. Jim patted Lady's head. 'Ah...you're being introduced. From now on, it will be up to you, old girl, to guard the baby at all times. Do you hear?'

Proudly, Lady wagged her tail. She would count it an honour to always protect this tiny creature to the best of her ability.

Another six months passed by - contented months for Lady who had accepted and welcomed her new role in the household. Although the tiny newcomer ruled the roost, Lady still continued to hold a place of affection in the hearts of Jim and Darling. But now, there was something more than just a nip of autumn in the air. Jim and Darling were packing suitcases and a general air of excitement filtered through the house. Yet, in spite of it all, Darling looked a trifle worried. 'I feel so guilty, deserting the baby,' she murmured to Jim.

'Aw, don't worry, dear. That should do it.' Jim snapped a suitcase shut. 'Got enough here to take us halfway to China.'

Darling had wandered into the nursery and was bending over the sleeping baby's crib. 'Darling...Darling!' called Jim,' we haven't much time.'

Jim ran to the nursery. 'Oh, Jim, I just can't leave him. He's still so small and helpless.'

'He'll be all right. Now c'mon. If he wakes

up, we'll never get away.'

'But Jim, I have a feeling...'

'Nonsense! Hey... what's the matter with Lady?'

Lady had followed Jim and Darling into the nursery and formed the opinion that for some unknown reason, they were running out on the baby. She backed away from Jim's caress. 'Aw, don't worry, old girl,' explained Jim. 'We'll be back in a few days.'

'And Aunt Sarah will be here,' said Darling.

'And with you here to help her - well, there's the old girl arriving now!' Jim paused to fondle Lady's ears and then rushed downstairs to open the front door.

A few seconds later, a middle-aged, rather dumpy person entered the hallway, carrying two suitcases. She untied the strings on her hat. 'Here, let me take your things,' offered Jim.

'Now, now, now, now, no fussing. I know my way around. On your way now. Mustn't miss your train. Have a good time and don't worry about a thing.'

Darling kissed Aunt Sarah's cheek and Jim picked up the suitcases. 'Goodbye, Aunt Sarah' he said. 'We sure appreciate this.' A few seconds later, the happy couple were hurrying down the front garden path.

Left to her own devices, Lady pattered up to the nursery, jumped onto the sofa and peered inside the baby's crib. He was awake and gurgling softly. Aunt Sarah bustled in murmuring, 'Now to see that big nephew of mine.' But she saw Lady first. 'Good gracious

— what are you doing here? Go on now. Shoo! Shoo! Scat!'

Hurt by Aunt Sarah's attitude, Lady grimaced behind her back and walked sedately away. From the nursery the croaky voice of Aunt Sarah floated on the air as she tried to sing a lullaby. It was a rasping sound and Lady was glad to escape from the offending noise, though it drifted along the upper hall. 'Rock-a-bye baby on the tree top... When the wind blows...'

Lady ran the rest of the way down the stairs. In the hall stood Aunt Sarah's basket. Curious, Lady sniffed at it, wondering what it contained. As she turned away, a snake-like tail appeared and tapped her bottom. Startled, Lady spun round to find herself gazing into two pairs of china-blue eyes.

Retreating to a safe distance, Lady continued to watch in frightened fascination. Two long chocolate brown tails appeared

through the slightly opened lid, swaying gently in rhythm to Aunt Sarah's singing. Puzzled and wary, Lady approached again with caution. The lid of the basket raised higher and two splendid Siamese cats emerged, stepping daintily into the hall. One of them tickled Lady's nose with its tail, then the cats started to sing in unison, even their eyes moving in time with their music.

We are Siamese if you please,
We are Siamese if you don't please,
Now we are looking over our new domicile,
If we like we stay for maybe quite a while.

The Siamese cats were very handsome with their brilliant oriental eyes and thick fur of a superb colour, blending from palest cream to the deepest chocolate hue. They were also highly unpredictable. Wearing smug expressions they tore into the living room. Lady followed at a discreet distance - these beautiful, tempestuous creatures were an unknown element in her life. Suddenly, one of the cats gave an upward leap and Lady's heart lurched violently. The Siamese had designs on the canary in the cage... evil designs! The bird fluttered, squawking in terror. Quick as a flash, Lady charged at the cat. Licking its lips, the cat slyly jumped onto the sofa where it was joined by the other one. Their expressions seemed to say, 'Later will do' and Lady knew the bird was in danger.

'Well,' said one cat to the other. 'What next?'

'The piano, it looks like fun.'

Within seconds, the two cats had sprung lightly onto the top of the piano. One of them slid on the highly polished surface upsetting a precious vase. It teetered on the edge then fell to the floor, smashing into a hundred fragments.

Lady was horrified. It was Darling's favourite vase. Water formed a puddle on the carpet and the flowers lay in a pathetic heap. Uncaring, the other cat raced along the keyboard producing a series of musical notes in its flight. Lady barked sharp disapproval but the Siamese cats ignored her. They next jumped to the top of the china cabinet and from that vantage point, spotted the goldfish bowl on the table.

'Miaow... do you see that thing swimming round and round?'

The other cat grinned, a wicked grin. 'Yes! A delicious, tempting morsal.'

'Maybe we could reach in and make it drown!'

'A brilliant idea. Come on!' With mighty leaps, the two cats sprang at the curtains, slid downwards ripping the material, then crouched behind a chair furtively eyeing their intended victim.

By now, Lady was thoroughly alarmed. First an attack on the bird... now the goldfish. 'Oh,' she thought, 'if only Jim and Darling would come back.' But by now, they were far away and Lady knew it was up to her to do what she could to protect all property from the two cats. They were destructive, intent on creating havoc. Lady summed them up as 'demolition experts.'

Padding beneath the table, Lady waited for action. She did not have to wait very long. One cat tugged at the long silk fringes on the table runner. The other cat dashed forward to join in the fun, aware that the goldfish bowl stood in the centre of the runner. 'There will be a head, for you,' sung one Siamese.

'And a tail for me,' sung the other.

'Not if I can help it,' thought Lady, grimly tugging with her sharp teeth on the opposite end of the fringed runner. A tug of war commenced. The poor goldfish swam round in terror as its watery home was jerked first one way, then the other. The situation had to end in tragedy... and it did! The two cats pulled in unison at one end, their sharp claws helping. Frantically, Lady pulled in the other direction. The bowl slid across the table top, swayed perilously - and then the law of gravity won. It fell to the floor with a resounding crash, flinging the luckless goldfish onto the carpet, close to the cats. They had retreated temporarily to the shelter of a chair but as the fish landed close to their noses, one of them rushed forward and picked up the goldfish. It floundered and struggled and, because it was so slippery, managed to flop free. But only for a second. Lady grabbed it, holding it gently in her mouth. For a few hectic seconds, the goldfish's life hung in the balance as the cats gave chase.

Lusty howling from the nursery saved the goldfish. Abruptly, the two cats skidded to a halt, their attention diverted.

'Do you hear what I hear?' miaowed one of them.

The other cat started to purr... a rhythmic sound like a motor running. 'A baby cry!'

Lady seized the opportunity to drop the gasping goldfish into what water still remained at the bottom of its overturned bowl. bowl.

With smug, self-satisfied looks the cats continued their little song, making it a duet.

Purr... a baby cry!
Where we finding baby,
There are milk nearby.
If we look in baby buggy
There could be
Plenty milk for you,
And also some for me!

The baby continued crying and the cats padded on velvety paws towards the stairs. A warning bell sounded in Lady's head. The baby... the cats were going to attack the baby. They must be stopped at all costs. Without pause, she flung herself after the intruders, mounted the stairs ahead of them growled, bared her teeth and barred their way. Enraged, the two cats had the good sense to realise that Lady was not playing games. She meant busines.

Discretion being the better part of valour, they retreated to the living room - now a complete shambles after their recent escapades. With a loud yelp, Lady gave chase. The cats sprang onto the window-sill frantically clawing at the curtains. Their combined weight brought the curtains down and they fell on top of Lady. Seeking to untangle herself from their heavy folds, she crashed into a picture stand. As it also fell to the floor, the noise reverberated through the entire house.

'That's done it!' commented one of the cats. 'Quickly, assume an innocent expression. Aunt Sarah must have heard that — even above her cracked voice.'

Right on cue, Aunt Sarah called out, 'Whatever is going on down there?' She sounded irritable and the two conspiring cats pressed close to each other, putting on an act of being scared.

After a frantic struggle, Lady managed to untangle herself. She emerged from the debris of torn curtains, smashed picture and stand as Aunt Sarah walked in on the scene. 'Oh, merciful heavens!' she shrieked in horror. 'And my darlings! My precious pets! Oh... oh, that *wicked* animal.' She glared at Lady, then scooped the two cats into her arms, where they sat as docile as innocent lambs. Aunt Sarah stomped towards the stairway. 'I will take you both to my bedroom for safety until I've dealt with this situation. Attacking my poor, sweet angels!' With another scowl in Lady's direction she climbed the stairs with her furry charges. Behind her back, they clasped their long, chocolate tails in silent congratulations.

Lady, crestfallen, dejected and sadly misjudged, sat miserably amongst the chaos. What had begun as a perfectly normal day had ended in disaster. How, she wondered, would Jock and Trusty sum up this situation?

Lady was not given the opportunity to call on Jock and Trusty and discuss the crisis which had arisen. Aunt Sarah had returned to the living room, her face grim. 'Now,' she said, roughly fastening Lady's leash to her collar, 'I'll fix you, my girl!'

Puzzled, Lady found herself being pulled from the house and down the front path. On the far side of the village green, an irate Aunt Sarah flagged down a passing trolley. 'The pet shop,' she snapped at the conductor as she climbed aboard.

Lady cowered on the floor, shivering miserably. When the trolley stopped, Aunt Sarah got off, dragging Lady behind her. The interior of the pet shop smelled of straw and biscuits; puppies yapped and kittens miaowed, while rabbits in hutches munched silently on cabbage stalkes and leaves. It was all rather depressing and Lady wished she was at home.

A clerk came forward. 'Good afternoon, ma'am' he said politely. 'What can I do for you?'

Aunt Sarah's face was red and determined. 'I want a muzzle... a good strong muzzle.'

'Ah yes, ma'am. Now here's our latest combination leash and muzzle.' He lifted Lady onto the counter. 'Now, we'll just slip it on like this and.. ah no...no...no...' Lady struggled violently as he attempted to fasten it. Violently jerking her head she slithered along the counter, upsetting bottles and a pile of books which slid to the floor.

'No...nice doggie, stop wriggling' cried the clerk, trying in vain to hold Lady down. Terrified, she leapt off the counter.

'Lady... quiet!' ordered Aunt Sarah in a very stern voice. 'Careful!' roared the clerk. 'Why...you little...' His words were lost as Lady's leash caught in the wire of a birdcage and with a resounding crash it hit the ground. Lady, by now thoroughly panic-stricken, dodged between Aunt Sarah's legs. Aunt Sarah made a frantic grab but fell over the leash and the birdcage. All the

puppies had set up a loud howling... the kittens were crying. Even the rabbits had stopped chewing and were eyeing the disorder with large, unblinking eyes.

Lady dashed the length of the pet shop dragging the birdcage after her. Emerging from the front door, she managed to shake it free. Without a backward glance she bounded into the busy street, Aunt Sarah's piercing scream ringing in her ears. 'Come back, Lady... come back here!'

Lady, still wearing the dreaded muzzle, shot in amongst the traffic. Horns blared as she rang underneath the wheels of a car and dodged a bicycle and a truck which belched a cloud of black smoke. Terrified, heedless of direction, she ran and ran until her heart was pounding and she felt that she couldn't go another step. She was lost, but at the moment that hardly seemed to matter. Tin cans caught on her leash as she ran, dragging noisily behind her.

She found herself in an alley but the noise of the cans had attracted the unwelcome attention of several other dogs. They began to chase her. Panic-stricken, Lady dashed under a bridge and across the railroad tracks, then under a stationary freight train. So for the first time in her life, Lady found herself on the 'wrong side' of the tracks.

Tramp, the lovable mongrel, was enjoying his evening meal. It was on a tin plate outside the watchman's hut. He stared in surprise as Lady flew past with several dogs in pursuit. Within seconds all of them had rounded a corner.

Tramp had recognised Lady and in a flash he had jumped a fence. He knew every short cut in the area as well as he knew his own paws. Lady, not knowing her way, had unfortunately chosen a dead-end alley. When she reached the end fence she cowered against it, terror-stricken. Her pursuers rushed towards her, barking and snarling savagely. Lady shut her eyes. This... this was the end. But help was at hand; a brown-and-beige ball of fury leapt over the fence from the other side, landing between Lady and the other dogs.

Shrinking back, Lady watched as Tramp hunched his high shoulders and waited for the fight which he knew must come. The dogs approached, more cautiously now. As they leapt forward, Tramp was ready. He fought with skill and great courage, first at the bottom of the heap, then on top, biting, snapping, snarling and scrapping. Lady longed to help but she was badly frightened and exhausted. She had never been mixed up in a dog fight before and it was dreadful... just dreadful.

Tramp began to gain the upper hand. In another minute, it was all over. The dogs turned tail and ran away. Taking a deep breath, Tramp walked back to Lady. 'Hey, Pigeon... what are you doing on this side of town? I thought you... huh?' He broke off talking when he noticed the muzzle. 'Aw... you poor kid. Oh...we gotta get this off. Hmmm...' Tramp considered the situation.

He pulled the cans from Lady's leash, picked it up in his mouth and said, 'I think

I know the very place. Come on!' They made a touching spectacle as they walked towards the zoo.

'Well, here we are,' said Tramp.

'The zoo?' asked Lady, puzzled.

'Sure! Follow me.'

A policeman stood guarding the entrance. Tramp and Lady hid behind some bushes. 'Oh... oh dear...' said Lady in a melancholy voice.

'What's the matter, Pige?' enquired Tramp, abbreviating his nickname for her.

'We can't go in. It's the sign... it says, "No dogs allowed." '

'Yeah! Well, that's the angle.' Tramp squared his shoulders, ready for a challenge.

'Angle?'

'Yeah! Look... we just wait for the right moment... and here it is now!'

A professor, his head buried deep in a book, ambled towards the zoo's entrance. Cautiously, Tramp slunk in behind the policeman's legs and whistled. The policeman turned round and neatly, Tramp fell into step beside the professor, looking as if he belonged to him.

'Hey, you!' cried the policeman angrily.

'I beg your pardon - were you addressing me?' The professor looked indignant as he lifted his eyes from the pages of his book.

'What's the matter? Can't you read?' yelled the policeman in a bad humour.

'Yes! In several languages.' The professor's tones were icy.

'Oh... wise guy, eh? All right now, what's this creature doing here?' He looked sneeringly at Tramp.

Tramp assumed a begging position, licked the professor's hand then jumped right up into his arms. The professor looked completely taken aback. 'He's not my dog. Go away ... please ... go away!'

Tramp refused to budge though he bared his teeth and growled at the policeman. 'Not your dog, eh?' said the policeman, whose tone had grown menacing.

'Certainly not!' In his agitation, the professor dropped his book. Tramp jumped from his arms and picked it up. 'Ah ha! I suppose you'll be telling me next it was the dog who was whistling...' The policeman waited for a reply.

'I don't know.'

'Oh! So I'm a liar, am I? Well, you listen to me.' The policeman grabbed the professor's coat lapels. 'Resistin' an officer of the law! You're gonna pay!'

Tramp barked furiously as the two men scuffled. Lady dashed from her hiding place and within moments, the two dogs were through the gate and inside the zoo.

Tramp shook himself. 'We're in. The place is ours!'

Lady looked admiringly at her new friend, admiring his courage and daring. They passed the apes, the alligators and the laughing hyena. 'Hmmm... if any one needs a muzzle, it's him. Just listen to that noise.'

Tramp considered each animal in turn wondering which one could free Lady from her muzzle. 'There's the answer,' he said at last and looked over at a busy beaver.

'Pardon me, friend,' said Tramp in his politest voice. 'I wonder if you'd do us a little...'

'Busy, sonny! Busy! 'The beaver started chewing a log in half. 'Can't stop to gossip now. Gotta slide this sycamore to the swamp.' He grunted as he strained to push the log.

Tramp moved closer. 'Well, this will only take a second of your time.'

The beaver looked annoyed. 'Only a second? Listen... listen sonny. Do you realise every second, seventy centimetres of water is wasted over that spillway?'

'Yeah, but...' Tramp felt desperate.

The beaver spat on his tiny hands. 'Gotta get this log movin', sonny. Gotta get it movin'. Ain't the cuttin' takes the time . . . it's the doggone haulin'.

'The hauling. Exactly. Now what you need is...'

The beaver ignored Tramp as he continued to mutter to himself. 'Hmmm ... I'd better bisect this section.'

Tramp tried again. 'What you need is a log-puller!' When the beaver appeared not to have heard, Tramp roared at the top of his voice. 'I said a log-puller!'

The beaver stopped working and clapped his hands over his ears. 'I ain't deaf, sonny. There's no need to...' He paused. 'Did you say "Log-puller?" ' His voice was trembling with excitement.

'Yes!' Tramp started to laugh. 'Ha, ha. And by a lucky coincidence, you see before you, modelled by the lovely little lady, the new, improved, patented, handy dandy, never fail, little giant log-puller.' Tramp accentuated his words by tapping his paw against the beaver's chest. 'It's the beaver's best friend.'

'Ya don't say!' The beaver leaned back on his tail looking impressed. He moved towards Lady who looked puzzled. Tramp followed, continuing his sales pitch. 'It's guaranteed not to wear, tear, rip or unravel. Turn round, little sister and show the customer the merchandise. And it cuts the haulin' time by sixty-six per cent? Wow!' The beaver was impressed. He laughed, slapping his tail on the ground. 'Heh, heh, heh. Just think of that. Well, howzit work?'

'Why, it's no work at all.' Tramp jauntily picked up Lady's leash and hooked it over the limb of the log. 'you merely slip this ring over the limb, like this, and haul it off.'

Eagerly, the beaver eyed the leash. 'Uh, huh! Say... mind if I slip it one for size?'

'Help yourself, friend. Help yourself!'

'Okay. Don't mind if I do.' He inspected the muzzle on Lady's face. Pointing to it he asked, 'How do you get this consarned thing off, Sonny?'

'Glad you brought that up, friend! To remove it, simply place this strap between your teeth...'

The beaver picked up the strap, placing it between his teeth. 'Like this?' he asked.

'Correct, friend! Now bite hard!' Tramp waited, holding his breath.

The beaver bit into the strap, a deep, hard bite. It split into two pieces and to Lady's great joy, the muzzle fell off. She worked her mouth stiffly, looking pleased. 'Oh... thank goodness. At last! It's off!' Tears of gratitude filled her brown eyes.

Lady and the Tramp prepared to leave. 'Well, friend,' called Tramp, 'We'll be on our way now so...'

'Not so fast' replied the beaver. He

jumped down from is log trying to put the leash on. 'Ah... not so fast, Sonny! Heh... I'll have to make certain it's satisfactory before we can settle on a price.'

Tramp paused, grinning happily. 'Ah, no. It's all yours, friend. You can keep it!'

The beaver was overjoyed. 'I can, eh? I can?'

Lady smiled coyly. 'Uh huh. It's a free sample.'

The beaver bowed graciously to Lady. Then he looped the leash over the log and it started to roll faster and faster down a hill towards the water. It bounced in with a mighty splash. Lady and the Tramp stood at the top of the hill watching the spectacle.

Beaver's head popped up out of the water. 'Say, it works swell,' he yelled.

Tramp nudged Lady's shoulder. 'Come along, Pigeon. You've had a nasty experience.'

Lady turned gratefully to her protector and poured out her full tale of woe. Tramp listened sympathetically. 'But when she put that horrible muzzle on me . . . ' At the recollection, Lady's voice broke.

'Oh, say no more. I get the whole picture. Aunts... cats... muzzles... it's disgusting!' The two dogs crossed the street, dodging late evening traffic. 'Well,' continued Tramp, 'that's what comes of tying yourself down to one family!'

Lady looked at him with curiosity. 'Haven't you got a family?'

Tramp stepped onto the curb and scratched himself. 'One for every day of thge week. The point is... none of them have me!'

'I'm afraid I don't understand.'

Tramp sniffed the air. 'It's simple. Ya see... Hey! Something tells me it's supper-time. Come on... I'll show you what I mean.'

Tramp leapt lightly onto a wall. Lady

followed. 'Now, take the Schultzes here. Look in the window. Little Fritzie... that's what they call me, Pigeon - I make this my *Monday* home.'

Lady looked very puzzled. 'Monday home?'

'Ach ja!' said Tramp imitating a German accent. 'On Mondays, Mama Schultz is cooking der Wiener Schnitzel.' As he jumped down from the wall he commented, 'Mmmm... delicious!'

He next led a fascinated Lady to another small house. 'Now, O'Brien's here is where little Mike... sure and that's me again, Pige, I've lots of names... comes of a Tuesday.'

'Of a Tuesday? Explain please.'

Tramp put on an Irish accent. 'Begorra an' that's when they're after havin' that darlin' corn beef.'

They trotted further along the sidewalk.

'Ya see, Pigeon, when you're footloose and collar free, well... ya take nothing but the best.'

Tramp stopped abruptly. his ears

cocked. Music floated on the cool night air. 'Hey - Tony's!'

Lady was listening, too. Close by was a pleasant looking restaurant with a swinging sign outside advertising 'Tony's Restaurant.' Tramp winked. 'Of course,' he said. 'The very place for a special occasion.'

They walked towards it and Lady went to enter the front door. 'No. No. This way, Pige.' Tramp turned down an alleyway explaining, 'I have my own private entrance.' He hesitated by a wooden packing case. 'Wait here. I won't be a moment.' He scratched on the lower portion of the Dutch door.

A voice from inside, called 'Joosta ona minute.' Tramp scratched again. 'I'm a-comin'. I'm a...' Tony opened the door peering out without noticing Tramp.

'What'sa the matter? Somebody's a maka da April fool...'

Tramp barked loudly and Tony looked down. 'Oh... hello, Butch's. Where you been'a so long? Hey, Joe, look who's here.' Joe peered out from the kitchen, then stepped into the doorway with a big grin. 'Weel, what'ta ya know. It'sa Butch!'

Tony sat down on the step with a laugh and Tramp jumped all over him, licking his hands and face. 'Hey hey hey, Joe, ha ha, Joe, bring some bones for Butch'a before he eatsa' me up.'

'Okay, Tony. Okay... bones a comin' up.'

Tramp, overjoyed by his welcome, barked loudly and jumped over to where Lady was peeping out from behind the packing case.

Proudly, he sat down by her side.

Tony had followed Tramp and now he looked behind the box. 'Huh huh heh huh! What's theesa?' He called Joe. 'Hey, Joe, look'a Butch'a. He'sa gotta new girlfriend.'

Joe scratched his head. 'Well, son'a ma gun.'

Timidly, Lady stood up moving forward into the light. Tony patted her head. Joe laughed loudly. 'He's gotta cockerala Spanish'a girl.'

'Heh, heh. Hey, she's pretty sweet'a kiddo, Butch'a.' Tony continued to fondly the pretty golden spaniel. He looked at Tramp and said confidentially, 'You tak'a Tony's advice an' settle down with thees'a one, eh? Heh, heh.'

Lady moved closer to Tramp, suddenly eyeing him with suspicion. 'Thees' a one?'

Tramp looked embarrassed. 'Uh. Dees'a one, dees'a - oh... Tony, ya know, uh heh, he's notta speak'a Henglish pretty good.' Lady couldn't resist smiling at Tramp's imitation of an Italian accent.

Tony looked at Joe. 'They can 'a come inside. Now, first'a we feexa the table.'

Tramp was jubilant. This was more than he had dared hope for. 'Go along,' he urged Lady. 'Walk through the Dutch door. We're getting the red carpet treatment tonight.'

Tony brought a small table from another room and set it in front of a bench. 'Up'a you go' he prompted his two guests who lost no time in settling themselves side by side. Next, Joe carried in bread-sticks and a wine bottle holding a tall candle which he lit. Its soft glow cast romantic, flickering shadows in the corner of the room.

Joe entered from the kitchen, a tray of bones balanced on one hand. 'Here's your bones'a...'

Tony spun round. 'Hockay, Bones'a,' he cried indignantly. With a swift movement he knocked the tray from Joe's hand, scattering bones all over the floor. 'What'sa matter for you, Joe? I break'a your face! Tonight'a Butch'a he's a getta best in a house.'

Joe shrugged. 'Okay, Tony... you're da boss'a.'

Tramp nudged Lady and winked. Shyly, she smiled up at him. Tony placed a menu in front of them. 'Now, tell'a me. What'sa your pleasure?'

Tramp and Lady studied the menu with interest. This was an unexpected treat. 'A la carte'a, deener ...' suggested Tony, his face wreathed in smiles. He clapped his hands. 'Ah ha, okay. Hey, Joe! Butch'a he says he wants'a two spaghetti especialle. And heavy on'na meat'sa ball'a.'

Surprised and a little annoyed, Joe stirred the contents of a huge pot. 'Dogs'a don'ta talk'a,' he snapped.

'He'sa talk'a to me!' yelled Tony.

Joe mumbled, stirred the pot again and plopped a huge amount of spaghetti and meatballs onto a platter. 'Okay. He'sa talk'a to you. You da boss'a. Mama mia...'

Tony placed the dish of appetising food in front of Tramp and Layd, and their tails wagged with appreciation. 'Now here you are. The best'a spaghetti in'a town.'

Tramp and Lady looked at the food hungrily then both dived in for a mouthful. Tony started to play his accordian and sing in his rich, tenor voice and presently Joe joined him, strumming a guitar.

Lady was entranced as she listened to the music. 'Tuck in' whispered Tramp, helping himself to more spaghetti. The words of the song were very romantic and made Lady feel more bashful and shy than ever.

For this is the night, it's a beautiful night,
And we call it Bella Notte.
Look at the skies, they have stars
in their eyes,
On this lovely Bella Notte.
Side by side with your loved one,
You'll find enchantment here,
The night will weave its magic spell,
When the one you love is near;
For this is the night,
and the heavens are right,
On this lovely Bella Notte.

Stars shone in Lady's eyes as she took a dainty bite on a long spaghetti strand. Tramp leaned down for another mouthful and as they chewed, their heads drew closer and closer together. They were eating at opposite ends of the same strand. Their mouths met and Lady pulled shyly away, feeling embarrassed. Tramp smiled and nudged a meatball across the plate towards her, using his nose. Coyly fluttering her eyelashes, Lady ate it while gazing adoringly at Tramp.

At last their delicious feast was over and they said their 'goodnights' with eager barks and a specially friendly lick for Tony, before walking through the Dutch door and back into the alley.

It was a fine, still night and the moon sailed across the sky like a splendid ship amidst a pathway of twinkling stars. 'Where shall we go now?' asked Lady.

'I know somewhere special — a very fitting place for a Lady like yourself, little Pigeon.' Tramp led the way across town to a beautiful park. A lake shimmered with myriad reflections; fireflies danced in the lights from fairy lanterns hanging in the trees. Close by, a fountain tinkled musically as a thin spray of water cascaded into the air falling in a filmy mist onto a white marble statue of Cupid. It was a very romantic atmosphere and Lady kept hearing the words of the lovely song which Tony had sung to them in the restaurant. 'This is the night, it's a beautiful night, and we call it Bella Notte. Look at the skies, they have stars in their eyes, on this lovely Bella Notte.' It was a haunting refrain and hard to forget.

Tramp whispered, 'There's a corner of the park which we must visit.' Lady nodded shyly, then trotted daintily by his side. He led her to a large circle of cement covered in dog prints of varying sizes. His eyes shone with joy when he read a sign saying 'Wet Cement.' He couldn't have hoped for more. Hastily drawing the shape of a heart he placed one of his paws inside the heart, prompting Lady to do the same. Then they stood back to admire their interlocking paw prints. 'A permanent reminder of our wonderful night,' whispered Tramp, his voice husky with emotion. They stared at each other, love in their eyes.

Tramp gently licked Lady's face then silently, they padded along a leafy path past a pair of lovers seated on a park bench. From trees roped in creepers, large-eyed tawney owls watched their progress. Crossing an arched wooden bridge, they reached the edge of a lake. Swans glided past and Lady and Tramp gazed together into the water. Their reflections stared back at them from the light ripples on its surface.

'We must find somewhere comfortable to sleep,' said Tramp. 'I know the very place.' Together they sleepily climbed a hill overlooking the spectacular scene below. From the narrow, winding streets came the faint clip-clop of horses' hooves as young couples drove along in carriages and gazed with fascination at the moon - a glorious lantern in the sky. Contented, Lady and Tramp snuggled down side by side and were soon fast asleep.

Brilliant shafts of sunlight and the dawn chorus of birds awoke Tramp. 'It's morning already,' he muttered, opening his eyes. He looked at Lady, still sleeping peacefully. Sighing with happiness, he nestled closer and dropped off into a light snooze.

Half an hour passed, then the shrill, penetrating cry of a rooster wakened Lady. Raising her head she looked about in surprise. 'Where am I?' she thought. Memory flooded back. 'Oh... oh dear!'

Her distressed tones penetrated Tramp's dreams. He sat up suddenly. 'Is something wrong, Pige?'

Lady shook herself and started to walk down the hill. 'It's morning.'

Tramp stretched. 'Yeah, so it is,' he said matter-of-factly.

Lady looked concerned. 'I should have

been home hours ago.'

Tramp caught up with her. 'Why? Because you still believe in that ever old-faithful-dog routine? Aw, come on, Pige!' He looked at Lady, his expression serious. 'Open your eyes.'

'Open my eyes?' Lady didn't understand what he meant.

'To what a dog's life can really be.' Tramp pranced in front of Lady. 'I'll tell you what I mean. Look down there.' He indicated the town below. 'Tell me what you see.'

Lady followed his gaze. 'Well, I see nice homes with gardens and fences...'

'Exactly!' Tramp's voice registered contempt. 'Life on a leash. Look again, Pige. He indicated the mountains in the distance, the fields, the vast blue bowl of the sky. 'Look... there's a great big hunk of world down there with *no* fence round it... where two dogs can find adventure and excitement!

And beyond those distant hills,' he moved nearer to Lady, bringing his head close, 'who knows what wonderful experiences? And it's all ours for the taking, Pige. It's all ours!'

Lady and Tramp rubbed noses, then Lady drew her head away. 'It sounds wonderful!' Her voice was wistful, yet unconvinced.

'But?' asked Tramp.

Lady looked at him, her eyes sad. 'But who'd watch over the baby?'

Sadly, Tramp shook his head. He knew when he was beaten. Feeling deflated he said, 'You win. C'mon. I'll take you home.'

Silhouetted in sunlight, they trotted down the hillside together. Determined not to be morbid, Tramp started to sing the words of 'Bella Notte.' They were soon out of the park and back into an alley close to a fence. At the far end of the street, the Dog Pound wagon rounded a corner, unnoticed by either Tramp or Lady.

Suddenly a sly expression crossed Tramp's features. They were walking level with a chicken run and Tramp stood still, asking, 'Uh... not to change the subject, but'a... ever chase chickens?'

Lady looked indignant. 'I should say not.'

Looking devilish, Tramp started digging under the chickenyard fence. 'Ho ho! Then you've never lived!'

'But we shouldn't!' Lady trotted back to where Tramp was hard at work, dirt flying in all directions.

The hole grew larger and Tramp finally managed to crawl through. 'I know we

shouldn't. That's what makes it fun. Aw, c'mon, kid. Start building some memories.'

Still doubtful, Lady crawled under the fence after Tramp. 'But we - we won't hurt the chickens?'

'Hurt 'em? Naw! said Tramp reassuringly.

Lady followed Tramp as he moved towards the hen-house. 'We'll just stir them up a bit,' he called.

The hen-house was very quiet. Tramp moved cautiously towards the door, Lady close behind him. Her heart was thudding and she was not at all sure that this was the sort of adventure which she would enjoy. Tramp turned, gave her a reassuring wink and stepped inside.

The chickens were all asleep, snoring sonorously. 'Just look at those fat, lazy biddies. They should have been up hours ago.'

'Lady paused on the step, peering in. 'Cluck, cluck.' The voice came from close to the ground. Lady stared fascinated at a little red hen crouched on a low ledge. It had woken and its sharp golden eyes were looking directly at her. But Tramp had been unable to resist a low bark and instantly, the entire hen-house came to life. Aware of strangers in their midst, the hens cackled loudly, flying off their perches. Tramp gave chase and pandemonium broke loose. Panic-stricken, the birds squawked in terror, flying with a great commotion towards the open door.

Lady was forced to dive under the ramp for shelter as the birds burst into the open in a cloud of flying feathers. Trembling, she watched Tramp emerge looking smug and self-satisfied. Surely he was ready to leave now? But no! Tramp wasn't yet through having his fun. He dashed after the fleeing birds, their raucous cries shrilling through the cool morning air. They dashed themselves against the fence, then scattered in all directions. Tramp, pleased with his performance raced up to Lady. 'Some fun, eh, kid?'

Before Lady had time to reply, a loud report sounded nearby and the ground was torn up in front of him. He stopped short and looked round in alarm as a man's angry voice rent the air. 'Hey! What's going on in there?'

'What's that?' Lady was shaking all over.

'That's the signal to get going!' Tramp ran rapidly towards the fence where earlier he had dug a hole. Lady, panic nipping at her heels, tore after him. She scrambled through the gap while Tramp kept guard then he scampered after her. Another gun blast tore a hole in the fence. They ran on, not daring to lessen their pace or look back. Yet another explosion sounded close by, hitting a building and narrowly missing them.

'C'mon,' urged Tramp.

Lady's breath was coming in short gasps but she kept close. Tramp turned a corner, raced across the street, doubled back and leapt through a mud puddle. Lady exhausted and frightened, ran through the puddle, heedless of the dirt which spattered her golden coat.

'Whee!' said Tramp, who had slackened his pace for Lady to catch up with him. 'This is livin'... eh, kid?'

'Is it?' Lady did not sound convinced.

Tramp's nostrils quivered with excitement. He padded down a grassy bank, waiting at the bottom for Lady to appear. Then he streaked into a round culvert beneath the railway tracks. 'C'mon, Pige,' he called. 'Follow me,' and dashed on.

Tramp jumped a high fence but Lady was too tired. Instead, she scrambled through some loose slats and flew helter-skelter in pursuit of her friend. Helter-skelter... right into the dogcatcher's net!

The net closed over Lady, pulling her up with a sharp jerk. Gasping and shocked, she tried to fight her way out of the heavy mesh but her frantic efforts were useless. Instead, she was lifted into the air and vigorously swung round. In a state of bewildered despair she waited to see what would happen next.

Tramp, unaware of the catastrophe which had befallen Lady, ran on until he reached a tall billboard on the edge of the highway. Cautiously he peered round it, assuring himself that the hunt was over. 'You know, there's a little bit of the bird dog in all of us eh Pige? Pige? Pige?' He glanced anxiously over his shoulder. 'Pige? Where are you, Pige?'

He sat down to wait. Long minutes passed but there was no sign of her. Alarmed now, Tramp shook his head. Where was she? The last time that he'd seen her, she'd been right behind him.

Tramp ran back to the fence he had leaped. Not a trace of the lovely cocker spaniel! His heart skipped a beat. 'Pigeon?

Pigeon?...' he called. But there was no answering bark... only a gentle sigh as the wind breathed along the railway track.

The dog-catcher carried Lady to his wagon, bundling her unceremoniously inside. As he slammed the door he said 'You won't wriggle out of that, my girl.' He climbed into the driver's seat. 'May as well get this one back to the pound right away,' he muttered.

Lady, released now from the folds of the enshrouding net, crept miserably to the bars and looked out. Houses and shops passed by at a dizzy speed, and then the wagon went through a gate and stopped outside a dismal, grey building. The sharp jolt as it pulled up, flung Lady on her side. The moment seemed unreal... a nightmare from which she might awake at any moment and

find herself on the hearth-rug at home. But harsh reality stared at her from the ugly face of the dog-catcher. 'C'mon,' he growled, reaching for her.

From inside the Dog Pound, came a fearful howling. Four dogs in one cage had their heads together as they yowled the words of 'Home Sweet Home.' They were an assorted group: Toughy, a mutt of no special breed; Bull, a massive bulldog; Boris, a Russian wolfhound; and finally Pedro, a tiny Chihuahua. As the verse came to an end, Pedro placed his sharp claws on the wire mesh and shrieked out a solo version. Immediately he was finished, Boris the wolfhound took over.

One old dog with greying whiskers was trying in vain to sleep. Glaring all round, he covered his ears with his paws. In the next cage, a mournful-looking dog listened to the words of the song, tears trickling down his cheeks. A young mutt, pressed against the bars, wept openly, howling at every chorus. Three young puppies, forlorn and in a cage on their own, trembled with sad resignation. Most of the other inmates were whimpering or howling... and still the chorus went on... and on... and on!

Toughy paused for a moment and looked over his shoulder. Behind him, a Dachsund was half-submerged in a hole he was digging. He worked furiously, dirt flying into a pile behind him. The Dachshund paused for a breath and looked up.

'Hey,' said Toughie, 'hey, Daschie, how we comin'?'

'Chust one more chorus und ve're out,' came the breathless reply.

'Okay!' Toughie turned back to the group. 'On a downbeat! One... two...'

He got no further for the door suddenly opened and the guard appeared, leading Lady on a rope. The dogs stared, their mouths still open. Speedily, the Dachshund leapt from his hole, quickly filling it with dirt, sitting on the remaining pile with an expression of innocence. The guard came closer and Lady felt all eyes turned in her direction and wished the floor would open up and swallow her. She realised what a great gulf lay between the world she knew and this one. Overtaken by real disaster and finding herself a survivor... after a fashion... she still felt the situation was intolerable. Trembling and frightened, she was led towards a cage.

A young man wearing blue jeans appeared at the far end of the Pound. 'Put her in number four, Bill,' called the guard, 'while I check her licence number.'

'Okay.' returned Bill.

'All right, baby. In here.' The cell door was opened, Lady given a push, then the door slammed after her with an ominous sound. It was a desperate moment.

Lady found herself in the same cage as the unmusical quartet, the Dachshund and several other dogs. The quartet eyed Lady hungrily, and trembling, she cowered down, more frightened than she had ever been in her life.

Toughy looked her over, a wide grin on

his face. 'Mmmm... Miss Park Avenoo' herself!'

Toughy and Bull moved in closer. 'Huh, huh. Blimey! A regular bloomin' debutante! Heh heh!'

Toughy eyed Lady's licence sparkling like a jewel in the dull light. 'Yeah - an' get a load of the crown jools she's wearin!'

Bull scratched his head, laughing uproariously. 'Yeah!' he guffawed. 'Whatcha in for, sweetheart? Puttin' fleas on the butler? Ho ho ho!'

The two dogs laughed raucously while Lady shrunk further into a corner. But help was at hand. The hubbub had awakened another dog known as Peg. Jumping up angrily, she flung herself between Toughy, Bull and the shrinking spaniel. 'All right! All right, you guys. Lay off, will ya?'

Toughy faced Peg, a certain respect in his voice. 'Aw, what'sa matter, Peg?'

Bull cut in, 'We was only 'avin' a bit o' sport, we was.'

Peg sauntered over towards Lady, standing protectively in front of her. 'Oh, can't cha' see the poor kid's scared enough already?'

Boris the wolfhound moved closer, addressing Lady in a gruff but kindly tone. 'Pay no attention, my leetle orchechornya.'

'That's right,' said Peg reassuringly. 'They don't mean no real harm, dearie.'

Lady looked gratefully at Peg and Boris spoke again. 'It's like Gorky says in an old Russian proverb. "Miserable being must find more miserable being, then he's happy." '

Peg whispered into Lady's ear, 'Boris is a philosopher.'

Lady nodded quickly, pleased to have found a friend in these alarming surroundings. 'Besides,' went on Boris addressing himself directly to Lady, 'Leetel Bublichki, wearing licence here, that is like waving... you should excuse the expression, red rag in front of bool.'

Lady looked perplexed. 'My licence?' she queried. 'But what's wrong with it?'

'There ain't nothin' wrong with it, Dearie,' cut in Peg.

'Confidential like,' continued Boris, 'is not one dog round here would not give his left hind leg for such a knick-knack.'

Peg sidled closer. 'That's your passport to freedom, honey. Without it...' She broke off speaking as Toughy poked his head through the bars in a listening attitude.

'Hey! Hey-hey, you'se guys,' he whispered. 'Poor Nutsy is takin' da long walk.'

Peg, Lady, Toughy, Bull and Boris crowded together at the bars as Nutsy, a pathetic black dog was led past on a rope.

'Where is the guard taking him?' asked Lady.

For a moment no one answered as Nutsy was led through a door with a sign on the outside, saying, 'Keep Out.' It closed after him with a clang.

Toughy looked melancholy. 'Through da' one-way door, sister.'

Lady stared at the dirty grey door, disbelief in her brown eyes. 'You . . . mean he's...' She was shattered.

The Dachshund reacted with great fright, jumping high in the air. On landing, he turned his attentions again to the hole he had been digging earlier. Now he worked like a demon.

The bulldog looked thoughtful, his eyes travelling slowly down to his grubby paws. 'Oh, well, a short life and a merry one.'

Toughy scratched his back against the bars. 'Yeah, dat's what the Tramp says.'

Lady pricked up her ears, looking surprised. 'The Tramp?'

Bull shook himself. 'Ah now, dere's a bloke wot never gets caught.'

Toughy laughed, addressing all the dogs nearby. 'He's a given da slip to every dog-catcher in dis town.'

Peg leaned forward confidentially. 'You won't believe this, Dearie, but no matter how tight a jam he's in... that Tramp always finds some way out.'

Lady's reply was sarcastic. 'I can quite easily believe that.'

'Ah, but remember my friends,' warned Boris. 'Even Tramp has his Achilles heel.'

Pedro the Chihuahua joined in the general conversation. 'Pardon me, Amigo... what ees thees Chilee heel?'

'Achilles heel, Pedro,' corrected Boris. 'This is meaning his...uh...his weaknesses.

Toughy and Bull exchanged meaning winks. 'Oh, da dames! Yeah! Yeah!' laughed Toughy.

Bull chuckled. ''E 'as an eye for a well-turned paw...'

Lady looked indignantly from one dog to the other. This unwelcome news was agonising. Bull stroked his jowls. ''E certainly 'as. Huh, let's see. There's been Lulu!'

'And Fifi,' yapped Dachsie.

Pedro blinked owlishly from his mattress in the corner. 'An' my seester Rosita, Chiquita Juanita Chihuahua, I theenk!'

Peg leaned against the bars, shaking her long silky hair, a dreamy expression in her eyes. 'What a dog!' she sighed.

'Yeah! Tell us about it, Peg,' yelled Toughy.

Still looking moon-struck, Peg repeated, 'What a dog!' She moved forward into the light.

'Peg used to be in the Dog and Pony Follies,' whispered Bull in Lady's ear.

The dogs gathered round as Peg began to sing in a low, husky voice.

He's a Tramp, but they love him,
Breaks a new heart every day.
He's a Tramp, they adore him...
And I only hope he'll stay that way!
He's a Tramp, he's a scoundrel,
He's a bounder, he's a cad,
He's a Tramp, but I love him,
Yes... even I have got it pretty bad.

By this time, Toughy was swaying with the rhythm of the music and beating out the tempo with his tail. A pail clattered noisily to the ground from a low ledge but he ignored it. Peg continued singing, the other dogs harmonising with her.

You can never tell when he'll show up,
He gives you plenty of trouble,
I guess he's just a no-count pup,
But I wish that he were double.
He's a Tramp, he's a rover,
And there's nothing more to say,
If he's a Tramp, he's a good one...
And I wish that I could travel his way...
Wish that I could travel his way...
Wish that I could travel his way!

Lady looked wide-eyed and puzzled as Toughy shook his head remarking, 'Yeah, but 'e never takes 'em serious!'

Boris leaned forward. 'Ah, but some day he is meeting someone deeferent...' Lady listened shyly as the Russian wolfhound continued, 'Some delicate, fragile creature who is geeving heem a wish to shelter and protect...'

Bull interrupted, motioning towards Lady. 'Huh huh, like Miss Park Avenoo 'ere, eh, matey?'

Boris nodded agreement. 'Mmmm hmmm... could be. But when he does...'

Peg swished round. She flipped her long hair from her eyes. 'Under the spell of true love...'

Bull took over. 'The poor chump grows careless...'

Boris shrugged. 'The Cossacks are peeking him opp...'

Toughy, silent for a while, chimed in. 'Pickin' 'im up... and then it's curtains for da Tramp!'

Lady trembled, overcome with emotion.

'Oh, no,' she thought. 'Tramp mustn't grow careless - ever!' The idea of him being penned up in the confines of the dingy Pound was unbearable. She shivered with fright when the door into the Pound suddenly opened. Surely... oh, surely, Tramp hadn't been captured.

Dachsie peeped from his hole with frustration. Hastily, he flung back some of the pile of dirt and sat on the rest. The guard entered, accompanied by Bill, the young man in blue jeans.

'It's the little cocker, Bill. In number four!'

'Okay!' Bill walked towards the cell and Lady's dejected spirits flagged ever more. What next?

The guard stepped inside and reached for her. 'All right, baby,' he told her, 'they've come to take you home.'

Lady could hardly believe her good fortune. Jim and Darling must have returned. Everything was going to be fine, after all. She waved goodbye to he new friends who looked after her with envy as she was carried away.

'You're too nice a girl to be in this place,' said the guard, not unkindly.

The door swung open... the blessed door to freedom!

Overjoyed at the prospect of going home, Lady had her first bitter disappointment when she was handed over to a grim-faced Aunt Sarah. They drove back to the village in a taxi. Lady tried to thank Aunt Sarah for her rescue but her advances were met with an icy stare and a reprimand. 'Down, dog, down.' Lady crept into a corner of the cab, remaining there until it pulled up in front of the house. Then, with a yelp of delight, she scampered briskly onto the pavement.

As Lady ran towards the porch steps, Aunt Sarah said, 'Not that way, my girl. I have a special place for you.'

Perplexed, Lady followed Aunt Sarah down the garden. At the end of it stood a kennel. 'You can stay in the dog-house,' said Aunt Sarah. 'Go along... in you go!' This was not the sort of homecoming that Lady had looked forward to. Dejectedly, she stepped into her new quarters. But Aunt Sarah was not through. Roughly seizing Lady's collar, she clipped a long length of chain to it. 'That will make sure you keep clear of the house,' she snapped. Left to her own devices, Lady lay down on the wooden floor, dumb anguish in her heart.

A few weeks passed, with Lady still confined to the dog-house and growing daily more dejected. Life held no interest... no pleasure. She awoke one morning feeling more dispirited than ever. A low blanket of pewter grey clouds hung low in the sky, adding to Lady's dismal frame of mind.

At the garden gate Jock and Trusty the bloodhound were deep in a serious conversation. 'Courage, mon, courage!' Jock implored his friend.

Trusty sniffed. 'But ah - ah've never even considered matrimony!'

'Nor I,' replied Jock. 'But no matter which of us she accepts, we'll always be the best of friends.'

The two dogs cautiously pushed open the gate and walked towards the bottom of the garden. 'Now remember,' warned Jock, 'not a word about her unfortunate experience. We dinna want to hurt her feelings.'

'Eh, yeah, yeah!' agreed Trusty, his face full of concern.

The two friends approached the kennel. Lady was not in sight. 'Lassie!' called Jock.

'Miss Lady, ma'am,' joined in Trusty.

Lady lay inside her dog-house, fretful and unhappy. Her head was resting on her velvety paws and she didn't look up. 'Please! I don't want to see anybody.'

Jock and Trusty poked their heads inside the tiny doorway. 'Now, now, lassie. Dinna feel that way about it.' Jock was worried.

'Of course not, Miss Lady. Why, some of the finest people ah evah tracked down were jailbirds.'

Jock gave Trusty a black look. 'Quiet! You great looney!' He tried again. 'Uh, please, lassie, uh... we've come wi' a proposition for helping you.'

Lady's ears pricked up and she came to the door. 'Help me? How? What do you mean?'

Jock looked slightly embarrassed. 'Well, now, you see, lassie, neither of us is as young as we used to be.'

Trusty moved his head close to Lady. 'But we're still in the prime of life!'

'Aye!' joined in Jock. 'And we've both got verrah comfortable homes...'

Lady looked very puzzled. What were they getting at?

'That's right,' continued Trusty. 'Where we know you'll be welcome and appreciated, Miss Lady.'

'So... a... so to come directly to the point...' helped out Jock.

'And if you could ah... find it possible to ah... to ah... to... ah...' stumbled Trusty.

Lady shook her head. 'You're both very kind and I do appreciate it, but...' She broke off in mid-sentence. Were her eyes playing her tricks? Jock and Trusty followed her fascinated gaze. Jubilantly rushing towards them was Tramp, a juicy bone in his mouth.

'Oh, Pigeon!' he said. 'Oh, Pige!'

Jock and Trusty glared at the intruder

and Lady tossed her head. Then with one accord the three dogs turned their backs on the visitor. 'Oh... ha...Hi, boys,' said Tramp to Jock and Trusty, trying to be friendly. 'Anything new in the kennel club set?'

No one answered. He gave an embarrassed laugh, then stopped uncertainly. After a moment's hesitation, Tramp advanced towards Lady and dropped the juicy bone behind her. 'Little something I picked up for you, Pige!'

Lady whipped her head around, glanced at the bone then with a muttered 'Hmmmmmmph!' walked disdainfully away, nose in the air. Unfortunately she was pulled up short by the restraining chain attached to her dog-house. Attempting to look dignified, she sat down.

Demoralised by Lady's treatment and with his tail between his legs, Tramp walked to the front of the dog-house and also sat down. Jock and Trusty still had their backs towards him but he made a further attempt at conversation. 'Looks like I'm the one who's in the dog-house.'

Trusty glared, calling out to Lady, 'If this person is annoying you Miss Lady...'

'We'll gladly throw the r-r-rascal out!' Jock completed the sentence.

'That won't be necessary, thank you.' Lady's voice was serene and composed.

'Very well, ma'am.' Trusty rose from his sitting postition with dignity.

Jock followed him then turned to face Tramp. 'You... you mongr-r-r-el.' His Scottish burr ended in a low growl. The two angry dogs walked through the vine-covered arbour, noses pointed haughtily in the air.

Lady continued to sit stiffly erect, her back still towards Tramp. He looked wretched and forlorn. He had been snubbed and put in his place. He was an outcast. Even worse, Lady wouldn't speak to him. Dropping onto his stomach he crawled across the grass to her, pleading with his eyes. 'Aw, c'mon, Pige! It wasn't my fault...'

As he drew level, Lady altered her position, once more presenting her back. 'Humph!' she said again.

'I thought...' continued Tramp. Lady sniffed and tossing her head, walked away. Her chain prevented her going far and she sat down with a sigh. Tramp tried once more. Still crawling on the grass, he said, 'I thought you were right behind me. Honest! And... and when I heard they'd taken you to the Pound...'

'Oh!' Tramp's reminder of her terrible humiliation was too much. Sobbing bitterly she dashed frantically back to the refuge of her kennel, flinging herself inside.

Tramp stood up and followed more slowly. Hopefully, he wagged his tail, wearing a woebegone expression. Inside, Lady attempted to control her tears. When they had stopped she thrust he head out angrily. 'Don't ever mention that horrible place! I was so embarrassed... and frightened.'

'Aw, now, now, now,' said Tramp in a voice smooth as syrup. 'Who could ever harm a cute little trick like you?'

'Trick? Trick?' questioned Lady. 'That reminds me. Who is Trixie?'

Tramp had the grace to look uncomfortable. 'Trixie?' he asked innocently.

Lady stepped out of the dog house, thoroughly enraged. 'And Lulu? And Fifi? And Rosita Chicita wa... wa... oh... whatever her name is.'

Tramp, highly uncomfortable at Lady's questions, tried to bluff his way out of the situation. 'Ch-Chita-ch-ch-ch oh, oh... ha ha... yes, well, I - I can explain...'

'As far as I am concerned,' said Lady contemptuously, 'you needn't worry about your old heel.' Her big brown eyes, shiny as topaz, flashed angrily.

Tramp backed away at Lady's wrath, but stepped right into her feeding bowl. 'My-my-my heel?'

'I don't need you to shelter and protect me.' Lady came closer, almost thrusting her nose into Tramp's face.

'Yes... but... but... but...' Tramp stumbled over his words.

Lady's blood was at boiling point now. 'If you grow careless,' she steamed on, 'don't blame me! And I don't care if the Cossacks do pick you up!' She backed Tramp right up to the clothes pole. With an arrogant toss of her head she padded away. Noticing the bone which Tramp had dropped close to her kennel, she gave it a violent kick in his direction. 'Good bye!' she cried. 'And take this with you!' It fell with a clang into the enamel dish right under Tramp's nose.

Lady disappeared inside her dog-house and a heavy silence hung over the garden. The overcast sky grew darker than ever as if a storm was about to spring up. Tramp's face was a sombre mask. Completely wretched, he wandered forlornly to the tiny kennel door. But Lady wouldn't see him or speak to him. It was his moment of dismissal.

With heavy steps and a heavier heart, he made his way towards a loose board in the garden fence. Inside the privacy of her tiny home, Lady sobbed bitterly until her cheeks and paws were wet with tears. Fate had dealt her a cruel blow. She loved Tramp but she had sent him away because he was a rascal... a scamp.

Before Tramp stepped through the fence into the street, he glanced hopefully over his shoulder to see if Lady was watching, if there was even a tiny sign of a pardon. Her kennel door remained shut. He sighed heavily. She was not prepared to forgive and forget.

Despite her tears, Lady's ears were cocked listening for the sound of Tramp leaving. When the fence board sprung back with a slam she ventured to the doorway and lay down. Tears still shone in her eyes and she was very, very sad.

Tramp trudged along the street, feeling equally miserable. Suddenly, the threatened storm broke and a brilliant flash of lightning illuminated the area. An angry wind stirred the trees and the village houses were sharply silhouetted in an eerie mauve light.

Amongst bushes in a neighbouring garden, a sudden movement was followed by a pair of fierce, bright eyes peeking through the leaves. A large grey rat, upset by the onset of the storm, had decided to seek better shelter. It scurried across the street, peered through the crack in Lady's garden fence and squeezed through. It dashed towards Jim's wood-pile.

Lady, too unhappy to bother about the storm, suddenly opened her eyes wide as she saw the rat dash towards the wood-pile. Abruptly she stood up as the first raindrops splashed onto the thirsty ground. Her coat bristled and she growled. Rats spelled danger... she must drive it from the garden. Alert, she waited, her eyes glued to the wood-pile. The rat emerged, running into the open. Lady, barking loudly, rushed forward but her chain jerked her to a sudden, painful halt. Panic-stricken, the rat seemed to lose its sense of direction, darting past Lady and towards her dog-house.

Lady gave chase, narrowly missing its tail. It was within an inch of her mouth when the rat made an extra spurt of speed, scampered up the cellar door and climbed the trellis.

Tramp, about to turn a corner close to the village green heard Lady's shrill, anguished barking. Instantly he recognised that it was not just an ordinary bark... but a sound warning of a hazard. Pigeon must be in peril. Without a second's hesitation, he rushed back the way he had come. Perhaps he could redeem himself.

Lady, snarling ferociously, bared her teeth while keeping her eyes fixed on the rat. It was still precariously balanced on the trellis. It climbed... higher and higher... getting further out of reach. Lady continued to bark.. Surely Aunt Sarah would realise that something was wrong.

The rat, its grey coat sleek and glistening with rain, had reached the roof. It paused, then advanced along the gutter. Lady continued to yelp and howl. The inky bowl of the sky was lit intermittently with lightning, and thunder reverberated in the mountains like an angry giant. A light flashed in an upper window and the rat, startled by the light scampered in the opposite direction.

Aunt Sarah raised the window, yelling loudly, 'Stop that! Stop it at once!'

Lady, momentarily cowed by Aunt Sarah's fury, crouched down, remaining silent for a moment. The rat continued to move along the edge of the roof...Lady resumed barking.

'Hush now! Hush!' Aunt Sarah made another attempt to quieten Lady... but to no avail.

Lady's eyes opened wide with horror. The unthinkable had happened... the rat had crawled through the nursery window which was open at the bottom. Oh... how to make Aunt Sarah understand! But she was not in a mood to recognise that anything was amiss. Instead she ordered again, 'Stop that racket!' and slammed the window shut.

It was a joyless moment for Lady. She had done her best, and through no fault of her own, she had failed. Soaked, her golden coat clinging to her, she stood framed in the light from the window. That was how Tramp found her when he pushed aside the slats in the fence then rushed into the garden. 'What's wrong Pige?'

'A rat!' replied Lady, not stopping to question Tramp's sudden reappearance.

'Where?'

Lady made a futile attempt to break her restricting chain. 'Upstairs. In the baby's room!'

'How'll I get in?' asked Tramp.

'The little door on the porch.' Lady indicated the back porch where Jim had fixed her a private swinging door. Those happy days seemed so far away.

Within seconds, Tramp had vanished through the swinging door. Once inside the house he looked cautiously around. He didn't want to run into Aunt Sarah before his mission was complete. The hallway was deep in shadow and Tramp approached the foot of the stairs. So far... so good! Quietly, he padded up the carpeted flight to the upper landing.

Listening outside the first door he came to, he listened. Not a sound reached his sharp ears. He moved on and when he reached the second door, he knew that he had found the nursery. It was partially open and the interior smelled of milk and baby powder. He entered with caution. The curtains were pulled and the room shrouded in darkness. The baby was taking a nap. A brilliant lightning flash revealed the rat on the ground, close to the crib.

Tramp's hackles stood on end. Emitting a low, throaty growl he advanced, guided by the evil glow from the rat's eyes. The rat moved to a chair and the two enemies surveyed one another. Losing its nerve, the rat scurried across the floor and Tramp saw his chance to attack. There was a short, sharp scuffle but the rat managed to skilfully dodge away. Tramp gave immediate chase, pursuing the fleeing animal round and round in the darkness.

With extreme cunning, the rat doubled back, crouching beneath the crib. When it found its way blocked, it darted in the opposite direction. But Tramp was too fast for it and they came face to face. Manoeuvring for an opening, Tramp rushed in pawing at the rat and knocking him into the air. It landed on its four feet, stood up on hind legs and fought with visious desperation. The rat knew he was fighting for his life... and Tramp was a powerful opponent. The fight continued...

In the garden, Lady was in a frenzy of despair. What was going on inside the house? She tugged fiercely at her chain. Suddenly and unexpectedly it broke... and she was free. She raced for the back porch, the chain dangling after her.

In the nursery, the desperate fight continued. The rat jumped onto the chair, then a dresser. A pitcher fell with a noisy clatter... a chair overturned. The rat sought refuge on the corner of the crib as Lady arrived in the nursery doorway. Tramp leapt at the rat, missed and inadvertently, knocked over the crib. Lady ran to the baby while Tramp continued his pursuit of the rat. Pandemonium reigned as more furniture went flying to all corners of the room. Soon, the nursery resembled a disaster area.

Aunt Sarah was resting. She didn't like storms but now she sat up in bed. Something had disturbed her other than the thunder. A thin wail carried on the air. 'Ah...' she thought, 'the baby is awake and needs attention.' She hurried to the nursery.

Tramp, never a dog to give up, was determined to trap the rat, but misfortune overtook him. A lamp fell heavily, injuring his paw. He made a frantic dive at the rat, got entangled in the curtains and they fell on top of him. The baby stopped crying and clutched at his rattle, Lady licked his little hands and Tramp limped towards the two of them. In the semi-darkness, Lady looked at Tramp, her hero, with adoration in her eyes. He had saved the day... and certainly saved the baby.

A moment later, Aunt Sarah appeared. Horror-stricken she looked at the scene of chaos, rushed forward and snatched up the baby. Lady and Tramp exchanged happy smiles. This was *their* special moment... a moment for praise and appreciation!

'Oh... merciful heavens! Oh, oh, you poor little darling! Now, now, now, now!' Lady and Tramp waited patiently... their turn would come.

'Thank goodness you're not hurt' she murmured to the baby, righting his crib and placing him inside. Then with a tirade of abuse and the pent-up fury of a cyclone she turned her attention to the surprised dogs. 'You... you vicious brutes!' To add emphasis to her angry words she fetched a broom from a cupboard, swished it at Tramp, saying 'Back! Get back!' She forced him into a cupboard firmly closing the door on him. 'Now,' said Aunt Sarah,' the Pound! That's it... I'll call the Pound!'

Those dreaded words fell on Lady's ears like the crack of doom. Her darling Tramp to be sent to the Pound ... enclosed, imprisoned in a pen after his heroic gesture. She barked angry protests but Aunt Sarah trod on the end of her chain, picked it up and dragged Lady down the stairs. Lady protested, howling and pulling furiously but it was useless. Aunt Sarah hadn't a sympathetic bone in her body as far as dogs were concerned. 'Come on! Come on! I'll call them this minute. I couldn't rest with that brute in the house.'

Opening the cellar, Aunt Sarah roughly shoved Lady through the entrance. The push sent her flying down several stairs but she rushed back to the top, reaching it as the door slammed in her face. She stood on the top steps whining and barking, but her pleas were ignored. Remembering the cellar's second exit she scampered across to it. That too, was tight shut.

Straining her ears she could hear Aunt Sarah speaking. 'I don't care if you are alone there, young man. I insist... I insist you pick him up immediately.' There was the unmistakable sound of the telephone receiver being replaced.

Poor Lady's heart almost stopped beating with dread. Aunt Sarah had carried out her terrible threat. She *had* called the Pound. It was the last straw. Tramp... dear, brave Tramp was going to be picked up. Frantically she flung herself against the unyielding cellar door, scratching, barking and sobbing!

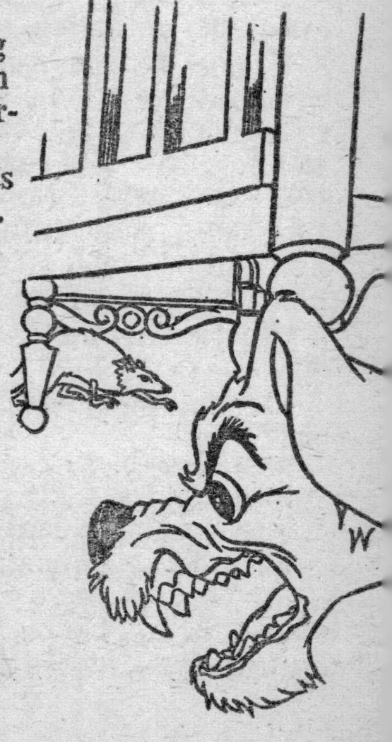

An hour passed... possibly longer. Lady, still imprisoned in the cellar had lost all track of time. But Fate was about to take a hand!

Outside, the thunderstorm had blown over, though by now the day was growing old. The first purple shadows of evening stretched across the gardens and streets. A streetcar pulled up close to the house and two familiar figures alighted. Jim and Darling had cut their holiday short. Jim looked along the street and stared in surprise at the horse-drawn Pound wagon outside their home. The front door was open and Aunt Sarah was silhouetted against the light.
light.

'Darling, look!' said Jim. 'Whatever's going on?'

'I've no idea... but we'd better find out.' Darling and Jim began to hurry.

Tramp, looking utterly dejected, was on a strong lead and the dog-catcher was holding onto it with a firm grip. Aunt Sarah was talking to the man from the Pound. 'And if you want my advice, you'll destroy that animal at once!' She glared at Tramp.

'Don't worry, ma'am,' replied the dog-catcher. 'We've been after this one for months. We'll take care of him.'

He tugged on the lead and Tramp limped painfully down the front garden path. He looked up at the evening sky and thought of Lady and the wonderful night they had spent together in the park. Now... he would never see her again. Once the Pound doors closed, it would be final. There would be no way out. With a sigh he walked up to the back door of the dreaded wagon and was pushed inside. The dog-catcher climbed onto his seat, picking up his whip to flick the horses. They were pawing the ground, impatient to be on their way.

Jim and Darling broke into a run, passing Jock and Trusty who were concealed behind some bushes, watching events.

'Say, what's going on here?' called Jim to the dog-catcher.

'Just pickin' up a stray, mister. C'mon... giddap! Caught him attackin' a baby!'

'Good heavens!' Jim's voice was alarmed.

'My baby,' shrieked Darling, tearing up the garden path. 'Aunt Sarah... Aunt Sarah.' Jim and Darling vanished swiftly inside the house.

Jock and Trusty emerged from their hiding place and walked up to Lady's front porch. 'I was certain he was no good the moment I first laid eyes on him,' said Jock. He had just seen Tramp bundled into the Pound wagon.

Trusty looked doleful. 'Yeah. Hmmmmm...

but ah... never thought he'd do a thing like that! Attack a baby!'

Lady, lying in the dark cellar sat up at the sound of voices, scratched on the door and waited. No one heard her and she stood listening. Aunt Sarah was speaking. 'Thank goodness I got there in time. There they were, crib overturned...'

Jim sounded puzzled. 'I'm sure there must be some mistake. I know Lady wouldn't...' He broke off to listen. Lady was barking as loudly as she could. Jim Dear was home. He opened the cellar door and she rushed towards him, licking his hands and face in welcome. The she dashed to the foot of the stairs. She had to make him understand - and there was so little time. 'Oh!' shrieked Aunt Sarah. 'Watch out! That dog's loose! Keep her away!'

'Nonsense!' replied Jim. 'She's trying to tell us something.'

Lady dashed up the stairs, poked her head through the bannisters and barked wildly to attract Jim's attention.

'What is it, old girl?' Jim raced to the upper landing and followed Lady into the nursery. She dashed directly to the fallen curtains. 'Lady,' asked Jim,' what are you trying...?' Bending forward he lifted up a length of curtain material. Beneath the folds lay the dead rat. It was obvious what she had wanted to tell him. 'Darling... Aunt Sarah! Come here!' yelled Jim.

The two women hurried into the nursery, startled by the urgency in his voice. 'What is it, Jim?' asked Darling.

Aunt Sarah peered over Jim's shoulder. 'Ah! Ah! A rat!' She shuddered in horror.

Jim stroked Lady's head affectionately. 'And Lady knew all the time. Clever girl. Thank heavens that she did!' For the first time in an age, Lady felt a glow of happiness... though the question of Tramp's safety hung over her like a black cloud.

Trusty and Jock had been standing in the shadows of the porch, watching and listening. When they heard Aunt Sarah screech, 'Ah! Ah! A rat!', they exchanged meaningful glances. So poor old Tramp was innocent — he had been trying to save the baby... not attack it. And now he was on his way to be destroyed.

'A rat!' said Trusty. 'We should have known!'

Jock shook his head sadly. 'I misjudged him - badly!'

Trusty suddenly rushed down the porch steps. 'C'mon. We got to stop that wagon!'

Jock hesitated. 'But, mon, we dinna know which way they've gone!'

Trusty was more optimistic. 'We'll track 'em down!' he cried, whipping up sprays of water as he ran through the rain-soaked streets.

Jock caught up with Trusty. 'A..a.. and then?'

'We'll hold 'em. Hold 'em at bay!' Trusty had discovered the wagon tracks. Jock kept close to Trusty, skidding and slithering in the muddy streets. Presently they came to the intersection, where many lines crossed and recrossed each other. It was impossible to tell one set of waggon wheels from another. Trusty tried his sense of smell, sniffing to the left and to the right. He looked discouraged.

'Now what?' asked Jock.

'The scent! Follow the scent!'

Jock sounded impatient. 'Uh, let's face it, mon. We both know you've lost your sense o' smell.' Nose to nose the two dogs faced each other and Trusty gave an indignant snort. He continued sniffing, determined to prove his worth. At last he picked up the scent. Baying loudly, he loped off into the distance, leaving Jock far behind. Jock followed as fast as his rather short legs would carry him. Down one street and up another, through puddles and mud ran the two friends. Suddenly they came to a section of roadway that was flooded; it posed serious problems.

Trusty ran through the water seeking to pick up the scent again. When he flung back his head and bayed, Jock knew that things were going in their favour. The search continued and they came to a steep hill. Jock's breath was coming in short gasps... he was not used to so much exercise. Then unexpectedly the object of their search loomed into view. The Pound wagon, some way ahead, was moving into a tunnel.

Barking with triumph, the dogs tore on with renewed energy. Tramp, peering dismally through the bars on what he felt sure was his last ride, suddenly perked up. Was it possible.... just possible... that an escape could be arranged? The wagon bounced frenziedly on a rough section of roadway as Trusty and Jock ran level with its wheels. Trusty leapt ahead in a valiant effort to overtake the horses, baying as loudly as any bloodhound had ever done.

Hearing the commotion, the dog-catcher looked down and saw the two dogs. 'Go on!' he yelled. 'Get out of here.'

The horses increased their pace. 'Easy boys!' yelled the driver, then to the dogs, 'Go on, you. Get away!' But the frightened horses galloped on despite being told to 'Whoa... whoa there.' Trusty's loud baying and Jock's barking caused the animals to rear up, their flailing hooves pawing the air. The dog-catcher made a last attempt to control the situation. 'Watch it! Watch it!' he yelled but his shouting ended in a wail of despair. The wagon swerved violently, then with a wild lurch, tipped over onto its side.

Trusty was not fast enough to move out of the way and as the wagon hit the ground he was bounced forcibly against the bars. His heroic efforts to intercept the Pound wagon had been successful - but he had paid dearly. Inert, unmoving, he lay stretched out on the wet ground.

Back in the village, Jim had been quick to realise the debt of gratitude he owed, not only to Lady but also to Tramp. At that very moment the luckless dog was being whisked to his doom. Jim didn't waste time on an explanations to Darling or Aunt Sarah but scooping Lady into his arms, dashed into the street and hailed a passing cab. A little later, the cab approached the tunnel which the Pound wagon had recently passed through. Lights from a variety of vehicles illuminated the gloomy intereior and focused on the scene ahead. A crowd had gathered round the wagon trying to calm the skittish horses.

Tramp, unharmed by the crash, was standing at the bars staring out at the chaotic scene. Lady, her head thrust out of the cab window spotted Tramp and gave a short, sharp bark. When the cab stopped she jumped out and raced across to Tramp. 'Hi Pige,' he said softly. It's sure good to see you!' Lady held her head sideways and Tramp lovingly licked her cheek. Shyly, she fluttered her eyelashes, her anxieties washed away. From now on, she could rely on Jim Dear to take care of everything.

But her moment of happiness was incomplete, for a pathetic whine caused her to look round. Not far away, Jock, mud-spattered and miserable, was standing beside Trusty. The bloodhound lay beneath the wagon wheel, his eyes tight shut, his body still. Lady jumped down from the wagon and ran towards the sorry scene, her heart thumping with pity. Jock tried to rouse his old pal, but there wasn't a sign of life!

Several months had passed since the unforgettable night of Tramp's rescue. Autumn's brilliant tints had given way to winter's quieter charm. It was now Christmas Eve and the village lay silent, its houses, trees and gardens frosted like a wedding cake beneath their blanket of snow. The sun, a blood-red orange, had sunk low in the sky; birds had sought the refuge of their warm nests.

Inside Jim and Darling's home there was a festive air. The tall Christmas tree, brightly decorated with tinsel garlands and sparkling glass balls, looked superb. On its upper branches a fairy doll holding a silver wand smiled down upon the happy scene.

Jim was making frantic to efforts to line up the family to take a photograph. It wasn't an easy task as they wouldn't co-operate and remain still at the same time. Lady had presented the household with four adorable but mischievous puppies. Three of them were tiny miniatures of herself, the fourth was an exact replica of Tramp, his father. Jim and Darling had insisted on adopting Tramp and he now sat proudly displaying his handsome leather collar and licence.

Jim and Darling's baby toddled towards him, waving a rattle in his face. One of the puppies pulled at the seat of the baby's pyjamas and he sat down with a bump, laughing and gurgling. Lady rushed forward, picked up a wayward pup by the scruff of its neck and replaced it in the basket.

Darling was watching the amusing scene and burst into helpless laughter. Jim gave a sigh of relief. At last Tramp, Lady, the pups and the baby were in position. 'Steady now,' warned Jim, peering through his camera. But at the last second, the Tramp puppy decided that *he* was not ready and scampered out of fogus. Encouraged by his disobedience, the other pups followed. Tramp dealt with the situation by quickly stepping on the naughty pup's tail, Jim suddenly yelled 'Hold it!' and the camera flashed. The picture was taken.

Jim, coughing with smoke from the flash, dashed to the window, flinging it open. 'Whew!' he breathed. 'Guess I used a little too much powder for the flash.' The front gate opened. 'Darling... oh, Darling,' called Jim. 'We've got visitors.'

'Visitors?' Darling ran to the window, Tramp at her heels.

Jock was standing at the front gate obviously waiting for someone. Then Trusty, walking very slowly stepped into view.

'Why, it's Jock,' cried Darling with delight.

'And good old Trusty.' Jim leaned further out of the window watching the two friends as they made their way up the path.

Trusty's foot was bandaged and in a splint so he was forced to progress at a leisurely pace on the icy ground. 'Ah, careful now, mon, be careful,' advised Jock.

No sooner had he uttered his warning when he felt a need to heed his own advice. He slid, slithered and fell flat. With a shake of his head he picked himself up. 'It's a wee bit slippery.'

'Yeah!' retorted Trusty, walking with slow deliberation.

Tramp jumped up and down exitedly. Trusty and Jock were now his good friends. 'All right, boy - all right,' said Jim stroking his head. 'We'll let 'em in.'

Jim, Lady, Tramp and three of the pups dashed towards the front door. The baby attempted to crawl after them but the Tramp puppy pulled at the drop-seat of his pyjamas. Darling picked up the baby... the baby scooped up the puppy.

'No... no... young man. You're going to take a nap.' Darling placed the pup back on the floor and crooning softly, carried the baby up to the nursery.

Jim opened the street door. 'Well, Merry Christmas,' he greeted the two callers. 'Come in... come in. I'll see about refreshments.' He called up the stairs, 'Darling! Where'd you put the dog biscuits? You know, the box Aunt Sarah sent for Christmas?'

'In the kitchen, Jim dear,' came the reply.

The four puppies, pleased at having new playmates made Jock their target for scuffle and play. After a while, three of them lined themselves up in front of Trusty examining with interest the splint he was wearing. 'Uh, no doubt about it,' Trusty was saying, 'they've got their mother's eyes.'

The Tramp puppy had found a new pleasure. He was tugging vigorously at the strings of Jock's plaid jacket which was a Christmas present. 'Aye!' commented Jock. 'But there's a bit o' their father in them too! The rascals!' With his hind foot he pushed the Tramp puppy away.

Lady and Tramp stood happily side by side, looking proudly at their family. 'Well,' said Jock addressing Tramp, 'I see you finally acquired a collar.'

Tramp looked bashful, scratching himself and not wanting to show how proud he really was. 'Heh... yes. Complete with licence.'

Jock nodded with pleasure, pleased at his friend's good fortune and quite unaware that his jacket was being unravelled by one of the pups.

Trusty moved forward. 'Oh, yeah. A new collar. I caught the scent the moment I came into the house.' He sat down. 'Trusty, ah says to myself, Trusty, somebody is wearin' a new collar. 'Course... mah sense of smell is very highly developed. Runs in the family, ya know!'

Jock smiled at Trusty and winked at Lady and Tramp. 'Hmmmm . . . there'll be no living with old Trusty from now on.'

Trusty grinned and the four pups lined up

in front of him as he began his familiar story. 'As mah granpappy, Ol' Reliable used to say... er, don't recollect if ah've ever mentioned Ol' Reliable before...'

'No, you haven't, Uncle Trusty,' piped up two of the puppies in unison.

Trusty pitched into his tale with gusto. 'Huh — ah haven't? Well, er, as Ol' Reliable used to say — he'd say . . . ah . . . ah . . . he'd say . . . uh . . . er . . .' Trusty sat down heavily, a puzzled expression on his long face. The pups wagged their tails eagerly waiting to hear Ol' Reliable's wisdom. 'Uh ... er...' After another attempt, Trusty was forced to give up. Looking acutely embarrassed he muttered, 'Hmmmmm! Doggone, he-heh. You know ah . . . ah clean forgot what it was he used to say!'

Lady, Tramp and Jock all chuckled, and the puppies resumed their mischievous antics, tugging at Trusty's ears and chasing round and round the Christmas tree. Outside, the snow continued to drift lazily earthwards, large snow-flakes the size of silver dollars. In the village the lyrical voices of carol singers were raised in their message of goodwill. 'Peace my children . . . love and peace.' Christmas tree candles flickered softly in lighted windows and the joy of Christmas reigned supreme.